Beat Sales BURNOUT

MAXIMIZE SALES, MINIMIZE STRESS

Stephan Schiffman

President, D.E.I. Management Group

Adams Media
Avon, Massachusetts

Published by Adams Media, an F+W Publications Company
57 Littlefield Street
Avon, MA 02322
Visit our home page at *www.adamsmedia.com*

ISBN: 1-59337-155-1
Printed in Canada
J I H G F E D C B A

Library of Congress Cataloging-in-Publication Data
Schiffman, Stephan.
Beat sales burnout / Stephan Schiffman.
p. cm.
ISBN 1-59337-155-1
1. Selling—Vocational guidance. 2. Burnout (Psychology)—Prevention.
3. Job stress. I. Title.

HF5438.25.S3338 2005
158.7'23—dc22

2004013274

Acknowledgments

My thanks go out to all the people whose help made this book possible: Brandon Toropov, Steve Bookbinder, Lynne Einleger, Amy Stagg, Scott Forman, Tina Bradshaw, Alan Koval, Surendra Sewsankar, George Richardson, Stacia Skinner, Art Jackson, David Rivera, and everyone else at D.E.I. Management Group. As always, thank you Daniele, Jennifer, and Anne.

Table of Contents

Introduction x

Part One:

STRATEGIES 1

Beat Burnout Strategy #1:
Test Yourself 2

Beat Burnout Strategy #2:
Learn the Difference Between *Creative* Stress and *Burnout-Inducing* Stress 9

Beat Burnout Strategy #3:
Recognize When You're Feeling Stressed 13

Beat Burnout Strategy #4:
Monitor Your Diet 18

Beat Burnout Strategy #5:
Make Your Move! 20

Beat Burnout Strategy #6:
Breathe Right 22

Beat Burnout Strategy #7:
Get Some Perspective 24

Beat Burnout Strategy #8:
Give Yourself a Reward 26

Beat Burnout Strategy #9:
Set Your Own Limits 28

Beat Burnout Strategy #10:
Have the Sense of a Goose **30**

Beat Burnout Strategy #11:
Don't Be an Eleanor **32**

Beat Burnout Strategy #12:
Group Like Activities Together **35**

Beat Burnout Strategy #13:
Take Back the Morning **38**

Beat Burnout Strategy #14:
Develop a Success Ritual **40**

Beat Burnout Strategy #15:
Make Your Commute Work for You, Not Against You **42**

Beat Burnout Strategy #16:
Take a Good, Long Look at Your Surroundings **43**

Beat Burnout Strategy #17:
Go with the Flow **45**

Beat Burnout Strategy #18:
Ask Your Manager for Help **51**

Beat Burnout Strategy #19:
Find Another Point of Entry **53**

Beat Burnout Strategy #20:
Escape the "Rejection Trap" **55**

Beat Burnout Strategy #21:
Understand Your Own Numbers **58**

Beat Burnout Strategy #22:
Abolish the Sales Slump **61**

Beat Burnout Strategy #23:
Learn the Ten Commandments for Making Sales Slumps a Thing of the Past **64**

Beat Burnout Strategy #24:
Take Twenty-One Days at a Time **67**

Part Two:
BEATING THE HABITS THAT MAKE LONG-TERM BURNOUT POSSIBLE **71**

Burnout Habit #1:
Selling Yourself a Bill of Goods **72**

Burnout Habit #2:
Setting Uninspiring Goals **79**

Burnout Habit #3:
Not Tracking Your Own Time **82**

Burnout Habit #4:
Not Knowing What Kind of Day You Just Had **85**

Burnout Habit #5:
Failing to Engage the Other Person Effectively During the First Meeting **88**

Burnout Habit #6:
Buying into the "Vanity" Sales Culture **92**

Burnout Habit #7:
Doing All the Work Without Getting Any Commitment from the Other Side **95**

Burnout Habit #8:
Forgetting about Prospects Once They Turn into Customers **100**

Burnout Habit #9:
Not Positioning Yourself as a Resource 104

Burnout Habit #10:
Not Getting Feedback from Your Customers 109

Burnout Habit #11:
Making Sales Projections That Have Nothing to Do with Reality 113

Burnout Habit #12:
Not Making Peace with Your Organization's Tech People . . . 114

Burnout Habit #13:
Keeping Your Supervisor Out of the Loop 117

Burnout Habit #14:
Not Instilling a Sense of Urgency 119

Part Three:
INSIGHTS 121

Insight #1:
Professionalism Prevents Burnout 122

Insight #2:
Urgency Is Different from Anxiety 126

Insight #3:
Everyone Has a Corporate Career Turning Point 129

Insight #4:
There Are Five Stages to the Sales Career 134

Insight #5:
It Pays to Move Forward 138

Insight #6:
Salespeople Who Don't Burn Out Have Certain Personality Traits 141

Insight #7:
You Can't Do Everything 144

Insight #8:
You Create Your Own Truth 146

Part Four:
FOR MANAGERS 149

Beat Burnout in Your Sales Staff Tip #1:
Determine What Your Ideal Performer Looks Like—and Try to Hire Against That Model 150

Beat Burnout in Your Sales Staff Tip #2:
Recruit with the Live-Breathe-Enjoy Formula! 151

Beat Burnout in Your Sales Staff Tip #3:
Strategize for the Marathon 154

Beat Burnout in Your Sales Staff Tip #4:
Set Regular One-on-One Coaching Meetings 159

Beat Burnout in Your Sales Staff Tip #5:
Choose the Mentor! 161

Beat Burnout in Your Sales Staff Tip #6:
Establish an Eight-Week Coaching Plan for the Team as a Whole 163

Beat Burnout in Your Sales Staff Tip #7:
Understand the Transition Curve 169

Beat Burnout in Your Sales Staff Tip #8:
Build Training and Retention Programs Around Your Top Performers 172

Beat Burnout in Your Sales Staff Tip #9:
Choose the Right Compensation Structure for the Salesperson **174**

Beat Burnout in Your Sales Staff Tip #10:
Remove as Much Stress as Possible When It Comes to Making Prospecting Calls **176**

Beat Burnout in Your Sales Staff Tip #11:
Understand the "Investment" You're Dealing With **178**

Beat Burnout in Your Sales Staff Tip #12:
Learn the Criteria of the Prospect Management System **180**

Beat Burnout in Your Sales Staff Tip #13:
Use the Project Management System to Develop Forecasts Based on Reality, Not Guesswork **185**

Beat Burnout in Your Sales Staff Tip #14:
Make "Faking It" a Thing of the Past **191**

Beat Burnout in Your Sales Staff Tip #15:
Conduct a Call Blitz **194**

Beat Burnout in Your Sales Staff Tip #16:
Ask Questions to Get to the Underlying Reality of the Sale **196**

Appendixes:
Thoughts on Burnout Prevention for Telesales Professionals **198**

Online Resources: Stress and Burnout **204**

Index **208**

Introduction

This book outlines simple, powerful ideas for revitalizing a sales career, reinvigorating your outlook on your work as a salesperson, and beating burnout once and for all.

Why should sales professionals concern themselves with this issue? Just consider the following:

- In a recent year, salespeople left their jobs in unusually high numbers, surprising most employment experts. According to Sales Performance International, a North Carolina consulting firm that polled 113 companies, most with global sales organizations, the **average turnover among sales professionals was greater than double** the expected yearly level of 15 percent, and in many cases was between **40 and 50 percent**. Some of these departures were, as might be expected, the result of cutbacks of underachievers due to recession . . . but a surprising number, perhaps 25 percent, were *voluntary* departures of salespeople companies wanted to hold on to, but who opted for a change of workplace (or a change of career). (Source: *CRM Magazine,* January 10, 2003.)
- According to *www.objectivemanagement.com,* the yearly cost per American company associated with sales-staff turnover (including training, recruiting, and administrative costs) is an **average of $464,000.**
- **More than 90 percent** of companies surveyed by Professor Charles Warner of the New School University of New York reported

having some level of problem with "plateauing" salespeople who were **simply "going through the motions."** Roughly one third of respondents estimated that between 20 percent and 30 percent of their company's sales staff could be described in this way, and a significant number of respondents put the figure at over 40 percent.

Let's face it. Salespeople who are stressed out, disengaged, and "going through the motions" aren't doing their careers (or their managers) any favors. If you're reading these words, you've already taken the most important step toward claiming a new way of looking at yourself and your career. Now . . . keep going!

Part One

Strategies

In this part of the book, you get the lowdown on the fundamentals of burnout—what it is, what its symptoms are, what makes it possible, how it's related to stress, what the different kinds of stress are, and how salespeople increase the likelihood of experiencing burnout without meaning to.

Here, you'll find simple *strategies* you can use right now to nip burnout in the bud. By implementing these strategies, you'll have a chance to beat burnout *before* it starts to eat away at your commission check . . . or your career.

Read this "strategies" part of the book first, because it lays the foundation for everything that follows.

Beat Burnout Strategy #1

Test Yourself

Learn to recognize burnout and its warning signs.

> "There are no great men in this world, only great challenges that ordinary men rise to meet."
>
> —*Admiral William "Bull" Halsey (1882–1959), naval commander in WWI and WWII*

According to the Wholistic Stress Control Institute of Atlanta, Georgia, burnout is:

> A condition that evolves slowly over a period of prolonged stress; wearing down and wearing out of energy; exhaustion born of excessive demands which may be self-imposed or externally imposed by families, jobs, friends, value systems or society, [exhaustion that] depletes one's energy, coping mechanism and internal resources; a . . . [state] accompanied by an overload of stress and which eventually impacts one's motivation, attitudes and behaviors.

A slightly less clinical but no less important definition comes from Christina Maslach and Michael Leiter, who write in their book *The Truth about Burnout* that burnout is:

> The index of the dislocation between what people are and what they have to do. It represents an erosion in values, dignity, spirit, and

> will—an erosion of the human soul. It is a malady that spreads gradually and continuously over time, putting people into a downward spiral from which it's hard to recover . . . [If you become a victim of burnout, these things might happen:] you become chronically exhausted; you become cynical and detached from your work; and you feel increasingly ineffective on the job.

According to many experts, burnout occurs in distinct stages. The first stage is an intense or even compulsive commitment to carrying out one's responsibilities; in the next stage, the person is increasingly exhausted, and makes a series of choices that leave him or her feeling less and less in control of life. There follows a stage of alienation and dramatically altered behavior; this in turn is followed by a period of bleakness and hopelessness. Last scene of all in this strange eventful history is a complete emotional and/or physical collapse that may be marked by feelings of guilt, rage, or self-loathing . . . or even, in some cases, the inability to express any feelings at all. Obviously, this is not a great outcome for anyone who sells for a living. Yet the sad fact is that burnout is quite common among sales professionals.

This book is a survival guide for the sales professional eager to beat burnout. Before we go any further, let's take a few minutes for a short "pre-test."

Burnout Test

Pull out a pen or pencil and take the following test. Put an *X* on the line next to the statement if you could have said it truthfully at any point over the past six months.

___ I frequently (more than three days in a row) feel tired at work.

___ I find myself trying to leap over steps in the sales process. (Perhaps, in weeks or months past, you were concerned about establishing commonality and learning about your contacts, but right now you feel as though you have "heard it all before.")

___ I find it difficult to generate real enthusiasm about my job.

___ I have engaged in at least three conflicts that I could have (and feel that I should have) avoided.

___ I feel unhappy with my work or career, but I'm not sure why.

___ I have failed to hit key performance indicators for a protracted period of time. (These could be in areas such as daily calls made, total number of appointments set, total presentations delivered or total closed sales. The meaning of "protracted period of time" depends on your own selling environment, but for most salespeople this would be something in the range of a month.)

___ I have not bothered to track key performance indicators, even though I have done so in the past and know I should. (Again, these are indicators such as daily calls made, total number of appointments set, total presentations delivered, or total closed sales. If you have never tracked any of these activities, you should not check this statement.)

___ I often feel that my efforts during the day have no real meaning. (By "often," I mean more than twice a week.)

___ I've noticed that I have been putting off taking important actions that I used to do routinely. (Such as making a certain number of cold calls at a particular time each day, or completing required paperwork.)

___ I failed to attain an important personal or job goal, but I was surprised to learn that this actually did not bother me that much.

___ The same person (a colleague or supervisor) has mentioned to me more than once in a one-week period that I have overlooked an important detail on the job.

___ I find it hard to engage myself in conversations with colleagues about how to work together to move a sales prospect forward.

___ I am consistently distracted by nonsales-related activities during the course of a day. (For instance, you spend extended periods of time at World Wide Web sites that have nothing to do with work.)

___ I received an informal warning or was summoned for some kind of "heart-to-heart talk" with my manager. (This kind of heart-to-heart discussion does not refer to meetings that are not part of your organization's regular, scheduled coaching process.)

___ I received a formal warning or some kind of job probation action. (This does not include scheduled performance reviews, even ones that include criticism or suggested areas for improvement.)

___ I find that I am more prone than usual to common illnesses like colds and flu.

___ I have other unexpected physical symptoms, such as high blood pressure, rashes, unaccountable aches and pains, severe headaches, etc.

___ I feel as though I am working harder but getting less done.

___ I seem to have no sense of humor, and that's not like me, and/or I frequently find myself in an ill temper.

___ I went on vacation, but the time off did not leave me with any feeling of release or relaxation when I made it back to work. (In other words, immediately upon return to work, you felt just as stressed and/or anxious as you did before you left.)

___ Lately, I feel underappreciated. (If there has been, for more than one month, a recurrent conflict or "personality problem" with a supervisor who you feel does not give you enough credit, you should check this box.)

___ I find it difficult to make decisions on the job—although this is not how I would have described myself a few months ago.

___ I have completely missed three or more deadlines for preparing proposals or other sales-related materials—deadlines that I normally would have met.

___ I would describe my confidence as low; I feel a general inability to do well in areas where I once performed with confidence.

___ I can't seem to show up on time for work.

___ I keep running out of time before I get to the most important thing in my day.

___ I have overreacted to the first negative response or comment from a contact or prospect.

___ I have used an initial negative response from a prospect as a justification in support of the idea that today is "not a good day to sell" or "not a good day to call people."

___ I have found myself saying or thinking things like, "I don't have time to make prospecting calls."

___ I have forgotten to check either voice mail or e-mail for a full day at least twice.

___ I find myself running out of time to return calls.

___ I notice that I have been forgetting about important messages and meetings.

___ I notice that I have forgotten about important appointments and commitments, and commitments that I've made with myself.

___ I used to think of myself as very disciplined about time management, but now I can't really say that about myself.

___ I seem to spend an inordinate amount of time doing my expenses, filling out my commission statements, and performing other routine administrative work.

___ I have said "You don't understand" (or any variation on it) to my boss within the past month.

___ I have a substance abuse problem. (If you have not been able to stop using drugs or medication even though you want to, or if you have not been able to refrain from drinking alcohol, then you probably have a substance abuse problem—even if you feel you really could stop using the substance if you tried hard to do so. For help in dealing with alcohol or chemical dependency problems, see your doctor. You may also want to visit Prevention Online at *www.health.org,* an excellent Web site that describes itself as a "one-stop resource for information about substance abuse prevention and addiction treatment.")

How did you do? Review your answers and find out how many of the statements you checked off. Write the number in the following space:

____

If you checked even ten items from the above list, there is a very good chance that you are reacting unhealthily to the stressful elements in your work environment. You may be in danger of experiencing burnout in your current sales position. If this is the case, you need to take active steps to rectify the situation. The question is, what do you do about it?

The first and most essential answer to that question is a simple one: *Learn what you're really up against.*

Read on to learn about what unhealthy stress is (and isn't), and how it affects salespeople over time.

Beat Burnout Strategy #2

Learn the Difference Between *Creative* Stress and *Burnout-Inducing* Stress

Learn to put stress to work for you—the right way.

"Take charge of your attitude. Don't let someone else do it for you."

—*H. Jackson Brown Jr. in* Life's Little Instruction Book

A certain amount of stress is probably inevitable in daily modern life, and *definitely* inevitable for anyone who expects to sell for a living. Selling is and always has been a stressful occupation.

That's not necessarily bad. It's simply true. It is inevitable that you as a salesperson are going to encounter some kind of stress. The stress you experience over the course of a given year may take the form of a difficult sales meeting, a harsh reaction from a prospect, the decision of a major customer to move to the competition, or even economic challenges that threaten your position at the company or your company's survival. The big question is not whether you are going to experience something similar to one of these events—you will—but rather *how you will respond to the experience.*

If you are looking for a job where there is *no* stress, *no* challenge or adversity or tension, then you are advised not to seek out a career in sales. (Come to think of it, though, can you think of a job—any job you would actually want—that would involve no stress whatsoever? What kind of commitment would you be willing to make to that kind of job? It's an interesting question, one worth thinking about as you examine your own position with your current company.)

Here's a secret about stress that most salespeople don't know: *We get to determine what kind of stress we experience.*

The trick is to be in a position where you can *use* stress, rather than let it take control of your outlook on life. Stress, after all, is simply another word for tension, and tension is a force that can be used constructively and strategically—or experienced heedlessly. The "strategic" outcome is one that most superb salespeople master. The "heedless" outcome leads to the progression of increasing exhaustion—and, eventually, to burnout.

An inability to *accept* any kind of stress on the job means you're probably not cut out to be a salesperson. And an inability to *handle* stress intelligently, or to respond constructively to it, can lead to major problems, both on the job and off.

So, a major client calls you up and announces that your company is out of the budget for the year. That's stressful, right? Of course it is! The act of denying that such an event is stressful or unpleasant is neither accurate nor healthy—and it compounds the stressful experience, making it worse! Here's the important question, though: What's your *response* to the stress you experience when you hear this kind of announcement from a customer? Is it creative? Or is it likely to induce burnout?

The answer you offer to that question will determine whether you're facing a crisis or a chance to move forward constructively. Or, to put it another way: *The way you respond to stress determines the kind of stress you experience.* Let me explain exactly what I mean, based on the situation where the customer explains that you no longer have a line in the budget.

In this situation *creative stress* is the kind of stress that leads you to walk into your CEO's office and ask him or her for permission to set up a face-to-face meeting with the CEO of the customer you just (apparently) lost. Maybe if you can get both of the head honchos in the same room, you can rescue the account! And, in case you're feeling cynical about such a possibility, let me assure you that I have in fact worked with my own salespeople to rescue exactly this kind of account.

Burnout-inducing stress, on the other hand, is the kind of stress that makes you sit and stew about the terrible situation you now face, replaying it over and over again in your mind without taking any constructive action. In this situation, the worst possible interpretation of the event you've just experienced is cast in iron, and you're very likely to ignore or minimize any resources that may be available to you to change the situation for the better.

Notice that these are two very different responses to the same situation. Notice, too, that your outlook has everything to do with which response you give, and which type of stress you experience.

Creative stress is a tension that leads to some kind of attempt to build forward momentum in one or more business relationships. Burnout-inducing stress is a tension that immobilizes you.

Creative stress is a tension that leads you to ask someone, somewhere, for a Next Step. (A Next Step is a slot in someone's schedule that involves discussing how you might do business together; the most meaningful Next Steps are those that take place at some point in the next two weeks.)

Burnout-inducing stress is tension that you internalize. Long-term symptoms of this kind of stress include insomnia, pain in the back, neck, or shoulder, headaches of various degrees of seriousness, chronic fatigue, panic attacks, and heart problems. It is also common for people who are serious victims of burnout-inducing stress to have urinary and gastric problems, difficulty sleeping, and other physical problems. Even more sobering: cancer and mental illness have been correlated with exceptionally high stress levels.

Turning an opportunity for burnout-inducing stress into an opportunity for creative stress is not something you learn to do overnight. It's something you learn to do over a lifetime. And there are a number of simple strategies you can use and practice when you are faced with the (fateful!) choice of responding to a situation creatively . . . or in a way that is likely to hasten burnout.

Exploring these fundamental strategies is what this first part of the book is all about. To learn about the easiest-to-implement ideas for beating burnout, keep reading!

Beat Burnout Strategy **#3**

Recognize When You're Feeling Stressed

Develop an awareness of the kinds of events that make you feel stressed on the job.

"Ask yourself this question: 'Will this matter a year from now?'"

—*Richard Carlson in* Don't Sweat the Small Stuff (And It's All Small Stuff)

To beat burnout, you must learn to recognize when you are feeling stressed—and *choose* which response the feeling will receive. This is one of the most important "foundation principles" for getting into the right mind-set and responding creatively to the stress you as a salesperson encounter during the day.

You must learn to spot *exactly* when you are feeling stressed, and to recall what your habitual mental, physical, and emotional reactions to stress are. Often, we quickly visualize or imagine the worst possible outcome of a situation when we're presented with a new piece of information. This is a major contributing factor to burnout-inducing stress.

Now, you might assume that the simple act of picturing or imagining something is a purely mental process, but the truth is very different. In the split second it takes you to form a picture in your mind (say, of your boss yelling at you for losing an account), you can initiate what is known as the *fight-or-flight syndrome.* This is an impossible-to-ignore physical change within the body that prepares you to either flee from a scene of physical danger or confront an attacker with physical force. Since neither of these are great options in the contemporary workplace, the act of picturing or imagining bad outcomes before they happen is a major contributor to job burnout. Why? Because these negative pictures or imaginings trigger huge chemical changes within your body (notably an extraordinary increase in adrenaline levels and stomach acid) in a setting where you can neither run away or lash out physically at your opponent. Putting yourself through this experience eight or ten times a day is a recipe for job burnout—and for physical and emotional problems.

So, noticing your *immediate* reactions to a stressful situation is extremely important. If you make a habit of assuming the worst about a new piece of information, or envisioning all the painful or difficult consequences you assume (often wrongly) you will face as a result of the new situation, you must notice this habit and make a conscious effort to change it.

No, I'm not talking about "denial." Of course you should admit what is happening. Do not pretend that a stressful situation has not occurred; do not lie to yourself about your initial emotional reaction to it. A great deal of stress builds up when we deny what is actually taking place in our world. If you lose a huge account, it is normal (and healthy) to feel upset and even a little disoriented by that fact. Denying that there was any loss, or that you feel bad about it, is a recipe for emotional instability and long-term unhappiness. But you must also take responsibility for the pictures you place in your own mind that relate to the situation you will face, and choose pictures that support and sustain you (say, your boss congratulating you for doing your very best in a tough situation).

Identify which specific events are most likely to lead you to form powerful negative images or dialogues in your mind; identify which specific events are likely to leave you feeling overwhelmed or anxious. Do not pretend that these events have not taken place; do not minimize their impact. But remind yourself, throughout the course of the day, that you really do have a choice in how you to respond to them.

The idea is to avoid forming an unhealthy fixation on the negative aspects of any experience, and to make a conscious effort to understand what kinds of events are likely to lead to physical and emotional responses that encourage this kind of fixation. By changing the pattern—and the pictures and exchanges you put in your mind—you will eventually learn to change the experience itself.

Practice monitoring your physical and emotional state; practice replacing discouraging pictures with "best-possible-outcome" pictures. By doing this, you will be taking the first, and perhaps most important, step toward controlling your reactions to stress—and experiencing more creative stress and less burnout-inducing stress.

Try this: Over the next twenty-four hours, keep a written list of the events that make you feel stressed, both on and off the job. How did you respond to these events? What pictures flashed through your mind? What dialogues did you imagine taking place? How would you "direct" the internal movie that screened in your mind if you had it to do over again?

Finally, take a look at these tips for recognizing and overcoming stress from the Canadian Mental Health Association.

Eighteen Tips for Dealing with Stress and Tension

Stress and tension are normal reactions to events that threaten us. Such threats can come from accidents, financial troubles, and problems on the job or with family. The way we deal with these pressures has a lot to do with our mental, emotional, and physical health. The following are suggestions to get you started on managing the stress in your life.

1. Recognize your own unique symptoms of stress.
2. Look at your lifestyle and see what can be changed—in your work situation, your family situation, or your schedule.
3. Use relaxation techniques—yoga, meditation, deep breathing, or massage.
4. Exercise—physical activity is one of the most effective stress remedies around!
5. Practice time management—do essential tasks and prioritize the others. Consider those who may be affected by your decisions, such as family and friends. Use a checklist so you will receive satisfaction as you check off each job as it is done.
6. Watch your diet—alcohol, caffeine, sugar, fats, and tobacco all put a strain on your body's ability to cope with stress. A diet with

a balance of fruits, vegetables, whole grains, and foods high in protein but low in fat will help create optimum health.

7. Get enough rest and sleep.

8. Talk with others—friends, professional counselors, support groups, or relatives—about what is bothering you.

9. Help others—volunteer work can be an effective and satisfying stress reducer.

10. Get away for awhile—read a book, watch a movie, play a game, listen to music, or go on vacation. Leave yourself some time that's just for you.

11. Work off your anger—get physically active, dig in the garden, start a project, get your spring cleaning done.

12. Give in occasionally—avoid quarrels whenever possible.

13. Tackle one thing at a time—don't try to do too much at once.

14. Don't try to be perfect.

15. Ease up on criticism of others.

16. Don't be too competitive.

17. Make the first move to be friendly.

18. Have some fun! Laugh and be with people you enjoy!

From the Canadian Mental Health Association, *www.cmha.ca*

Beat Burnout Strategy **#4**

Monitor Your Diet

Give your body what it needs.

"You are what you eat."

—*Anonymous*

Maintaining good nutrition is one of the most important tools for turning an opportunity for burnout-inducing stress into an opportunity for creative stress. This is not a diet book, but it is meant to give you all the tools you need to overcome destructive reactions to stress.

Your body needs the right fuel in the right amounts in order to turn burnout-inducing stress into creative stress, so it's worth pointing out here that scientists have concluded that a deficiency of certain nutrients can dramatically affect an individual's unhealthy reactions to stress. Deficiencies in vitamin C, the B-complex vitamins, and the minerals zinc, magnesium, phosphorus, and calcium can make life less than enjoyable. A healthy diet will supply all of these nutrients, but if you are concerned about an insufficiency in any of these, you should talk to your doctor and learn about the advisability of taking vitamin supplements.

You should also consider . . .

- Eating three to five servings of fresh fruits and vegetables each day.
- Drinking four or five glasses of water each day. (Water is an extremely important component of a healthy diet, and is essential to the maintenance of healthy cells and tissues.)
- Cutting down on fatty foods.
- Minimizing coffee intake. (Many burned-out salespeople I've worked with turned out to be salespeople who had a permanent case of the jitters as a result of excessive caffeine consumption.)

Remember, you really do have a body. You don't just have a head that rides around on some vehicle that happens to have arms, legs, and appetites. How well your body does at the important job of handling stress depends on the kind of things you put into it.

If being "committed to your job" means skipping meals, eating unhealthily, downing eight cups of coffee a day, or ignoring clear physical symptoms that there is something wrong (such as obesity), then you are taking your job too seriously. See a doctor and ask for help in setting up a nutritional plan that makes sense for you.

Beat Burnout Strategy #5

Make Your Move!

Physical motion dispels burnout-inducing stress.

"You got to move."

—*The Rolling Stones*

The simple act of moving your body is a powerful weapon against burnout.

I'm sharing this principle with you very early in the book, so you can take full advantage of it immediately. I want to caution you *not* to ignore the powerful impact that physical movement can have on your ability to turn burnout-inducing stress into creative stress. Find ways to adapt this "movement principle" throughout your day, even though it appears in only a single chapter of this book.

The two simple ideas you're about to read are just as important as any other strategies I'll be sharing with you in this book, and should be kept in the front of mind your mind, always.

1. **Change your emotional state by changing your physical state.** Perhaps the most effective way to respond to a burnout-inducing stressful situation is to make a conscious choice to do something dramatically different with your body.

For instance, let's say you've been working on a proposal that you felt sure was the only one your prospect would be considering, but you learned that four competitors will be committing proposals as well. It is natural for you to feel unhappy. Once you have processed the information, however, you should resist the temptation to, say, slump over your desk and stare blankly at the computer screen.

Instead, stand up tall, clap your hands, and walk purposefully around your work area. Keep your head up. Make sure your gaze is upward. Do this for just a minute or so following the handclap, with full attention and honest effort, and I guarantee that you will feel a dramatic change in your emotional resources and reactions. You will be in a much better position to picture positive outcomes . . . and then develop a proposal that blows the doors off your competition.

2. **Take a midday exercise break of some kind.** If you have access to shower facilities, take a brisk jog for ten or fifteen minutes in the middle of the day. If you don't, grab a colleague and take a pleasant walk. Whatever you do, make sure that you find *some* way to elevate your heart rate at some point during the day. Exercise—even light exercise—is an essential weapon when it comes to beating burnout. A startlingly high proportion of the burned-out salespeople with whom I've worked have had problems with inactivity and/or obesity.

A side note related to exercise: Make "achievement" something that applies to all areas of your life, including physical workouts of some kind. See your doctor regularly. Do not skip sleep. Eat healthy food. Watch your weight. And do make a point of getting some kind of physical exercise at least once a day.

Beat Burnout Strategy #6

Breathe Right

A simple, powerful strategy that too many salespeople overlook.

"Breathe deep."

—Pink Floyd

When you feel stressed, take a deep breath. The simple act of breathing deeply has remarkable physiological and emotional healing properties and can help you overcome, or at least position yourself properly, for virtually any challenge.

If you have ever seen the film or videotape of James Whitmore's one-man show, *Give 'Em Hell Harry,* you've seen a character study of a president of the United States well-versed in the art of taking deep breaths as a stress management technique. (Whitmore's performance is based on close observation of footage of Truman himself.)

When the president faces a steel crisis that could cripple the nation's economy, Truman takes a deep breath before doing anything else. When the unions call a rail strike and immobilize the country, Truman takes a deep breath before doing anything else. When the smear tactics of Senator Joseph McCarthy threaten to undermine not only the United States Senate but also the basic democratic processes of the republic, Truman takes a deep breath before doing anything else. Truman uses the same strategy, via Whitmore, to come to terms with crises in Berlin, the Soviet Union, Korea, and the atom bomb.

As evidenced by Whitmore's remarkable, historically accurate performance, taking a deep breath is an important first step in dealing with stressful situations. It is a cheap, simple, and remarkably effective antistress tool that all sales professionals can use to cut off feelings of helplessness, anger, or impending doom—before these emotions harden into burnout-inducing stress.

The example of Truman is worth considering closely in another respect. If we think our day is tough, it's certainly nothing compared to Truman's (or any president's). We owe it to ourselves to take advantage of a tool that the thirty-third president no doubt used regularly to get through the day with his resolve intact, his attitude correct, and his burnout factor low.

Beat Burnout Strategy **#7**

Get Some Perspective

Follow the advice of New York Yankees great—and stress management expert—Mickey Rivers: Just don't worry.

> "Control your emotion, or it will control you."
>
> —*Samurai maxim*

When you notice yourself beginning to feel stressed, step back from the situation. Ask yourself: How important is this, really? Is it worth losing my composure over? Is it worth risking my health and perhaps my life over? (Unhealthy reactions to stress, as I've noted elsewhere in this book are in fact correlated with serious health problems.)

Make a conscious effort to understand what you likely can change in this situation, and what you cannot. Do not fixate on aspects of the situation that are utterly beyond your control. *Do not visualize these elements or imagine dialogues related to them!* Instead, identify what you *can* affect, and then be willing to change what is not working. Look for a way to address the situation that could incorporate a Next Step of some kind—perhaps a discussion or meeting with someone in your contact network at some point within the next two weeks.

Based on whatever stress you're facing, changing what is not working might mean calling someone else within the target organization; or it might mean altering your personal schedule for the day. It might also mean setting different kinds of daily targets for specific activities that you undertake, such as prospecting calls or proposal development.

So, let's take a specific example. Assume that an important client's budget has been reduced by 50 percent due to a prolonged national economic downturn. Now, mentally replaying the meeting at which the bad news was delivered to you is not going to help reduce your stress level. Focusing instead on those aspects of the situation that you *can* affect and *can* change for the better is a much better idea.

That might mean identifying an entirely new industry to which you have not been prospecting recently, or it might mean sitting down with your manager to brainstorm ideas for new product and pricing arrangements for the current client, or it might even mean finding new ways of distributing your products and services so that you can target a group of potential buyers that *isn't* having budget problems just now.

That "lousy meeting" where you found out about the budget cutbacks, however, is not something you can change.

The great New York Yankees outfielder Mickey Rivers used to say, "Ain't no use worrying about things that are under your control, because if you've got 'em under control, ain't no use worrying. And ain't no use worrying about things that *ain't* under your control, because if you *ain't* got 'em under control, ain't no use worrying."

Beat Burnout Strategy **#8**

Give Yourself a Reward

Find at least one point in your day when the most important item on the to-do list is to be good to yourself.

"There is always, always, always something to be thankful for."

—Anonymous

Many salespeople whose careers are sidelined by burnout-inducing stress have a tough time disengaging from the day. But it is extremely important to be able to relax and reward yourself somehow during the course of the day. The ability to do so is, I think, an essential survival skill for professional salespeople in the twenty-first century.

Remember that television show *Twin Peaks*, which was popular back in the 1990s? The central character, Agent Cooper, had a saying that went something like this: "Find a reason to do something nice for yourself at least once a day." This is, I think, mandatory advice for salespeople. No matter how important it is to be able to summon your own intensity, no matter how goal-oriented you are, no matter how important a proposal is, the conscious choice to take a few minutes to disengage from work and relax in a way that makes you feel whole is good selling strategy.

Find an opportunity to disengage and focus on something non-work-related that you love. Do this for, say, five minutes, at least once a day. (For Agent Cooper, it was a piece of pie and a cup of coffee. For you, it might be a call to a family member or a coffee-break slot of time all alone with a book you love.)

This "daily relaxation period" is a good opportunity to remind yourself how important it is to laugh at life. If everything is a crisis and you never have any fun, then sales is definitely not for you. The only truly successful salespeople in the long term are those who know how to appreciate the humor and whimsy of their daily lives.

Beat Burnout Strategy #9

Set Your Own Limits

Take charge of your day—and your career!

"When you are content to be simply yourself and don't compare or compete, everybody will respect you."

—Lao Tzu (c. 570–490 B.C.), founder of Taoism

Salespeople who are not prone to burnout, I have noticed, learn to set limits in their professional lives. Here are three simple steps you can take to do just that:

1. **Say no once in a while.** You do not have an obligation to let a given prospect dictate your daily, weekly, monthly, quarterly, or yearly schedule. *You* are in charge of your time and your attention, and *you* must make the decisions regarding the allocation of these resources. Before you choose to commit vast amounts of time and effort to any project or proposal, ask yourself how committed *the other person* is to working with you on this project. Ask yourself what levels of time and investment he or she is willing to make.

We have many business contacts at our organization who ask us to jump through various hoops in order to prepare responses to RFPs (requests for proposals) on major sales training deals.

A good proportion of the time, we simply decline to answer the four dozen questions that have been developed in the RFP document. We simply say no to the possibility of competing for that business. Why? Because the decision-maker has invested very little of his or her own time and energy in the process, and we have learned from bitter experience that there is a very low likelihood of our winning business in such a setting. (The only exception to this is the setting in which we have been working with a prospect who must, by internal rule, send a project out to bid, but is willing to let us help design the RFP to accent areas of our own strengths.)

2. **Do not take on a role in someone else's soap opera.** It is all very well to be empathetic, and it is certainly important to work together as a team. That does not mean, however, that you have an obligation to listen to every extended monologue of complaint, and it certainly does not mean that you should allow people to place work items on your list that belong on their lists.

3. **Delegate.** Different sales organizations have different levels of clerical and administrative support. It is unlikely, though, that even if you work in a bare-bones environment, your boss wants you spending the day typing up letters rather than setting appointments and getting out meeting prospects. If you need help, ask for it! See what happens.

Beat Burnout Strategy **#10**

Have the Sense of a Goose

Build a support network.

"Friendship is a sheltering tree."

—Samuel Taylor Coleridge, nineteenth-century English poet

Do you consider yourself a go-it-alone kind of person? Many salespeople do. If that's the case, you might want to consider posting the following essay, whose author is unknown, in your work station, where you can see it every day. Then start reaching out to form alliances with people you know and trust in your organization.

> When you see geese flying along in V formation, you might consider what science has discovered as to why they fly that way.
>
> As each bird flaps its wings, it creates an uplift for the bird immediately following. By flying in V formation, the whole flock adds at least 71 percent greater flying range than if each bird flew on its own. People who share a common direction and sense of community can get where they are going more quickly and easily because they are traveling on the thrust of one another.
>
> When a goose falls out of formation, it suddenly feels the drag and resistance of trying to go it alone, and quickly gets back into formation to take advantage of the lifting power of the bird in front.

If we have as much sense as a goose, we will stay in formation with those people who are headed the same way we are.

When the head goose gets tired, it rotates back in the formation and another goose flies point. It is sensible to take turns doing demanding jobs, whether with people or with geese flying south.

Geese honk from behind to encourage those up front to keep up their speed. What messages do we give when we honk from behind?

Finally—and this is important—when a goose gets sick or is wounded by gunshot, and falls out of formation, two other geese fall out with that goose and follow it down to lend help and protection. They stay with the fallen goose until it is able to fly or until it dies, and only then do they launch out on their own, or with another formation, to catch up with their group.

If we have the sense of a goose, we will stand by each other like that.

—Author unknown

Beat Burnout Strategy **#11**

Don't Be an Eleanor

A case study in burnout.

"The day a person becomes a cynic is the day he loses his youth."

—*Football coach Marvin D. Levy*

Three or four years ago, we had a "loner" salesperson who never asked for help and never accepted help when it was offered to her; I'll call her "Eleanor." In addition to neglecting to build up a support network, Eleanor had a remarkable habit: not working on any task for more than five consecutive minutes.

Eleanor would make a single prospecting call, then stop, hang up the phone, and walk into my office to tell me everything that had just happened on the call, either good or bad. When I encouraged her to continue her morning prospecting calls, she would make her way to the water cooler, have a drink, talk to a colleague for a few minutes, sit back down at her desk, straighten up the papers, put something up on the Internet, and then, probably ten minutes later, pick up the phone and make another call. Then, quite often, the whole cycle would start all over again.

In fact, I noticed that Eleanor would repeat variations on this process for most of the morning. For instance, she would find some way to engage herself in two sorts of paperwork at once. Or she would compose an e-mail to one prospect at the same time she was trying to set an appointment with another. When it was time for lunch, Eleanor would usually sit down across from someone else's desk and engage in a lengthy discussion about what restaurant made the most sense to visit. After taking an hour and a half at lunch, she would get back to the office briefly, check her voice mail, and then head out the door for an afternoon sales appointment.

Typically, I would not see her until the next morning.

This was Eleanor's average day. It should not be entirely surprising to you to learn that her total prospecting activity was unimpressive. Prospecting is what delivers new relationships, and new relationships are what eventually deliver new sales income. Yet Eleanor was so distracted, and spread out in so many different directions, that she never managed to hit her quota for first appointments—and she never managed to accumulate much in the way of new commission income. (She had a few long-term accounts that she had inherited from another salesperson, and these relationship-driven accounts brought her some income. But the main part of her job—finding new customers—was fatally neglected.)

The bottom line is this: The name of the game in our company is to track down new business, and Eleanor really didn't have much success at that. I had to ask myself: *Why?*

Here was my answer. The *reason* she didn't have much success at attracting new customers was that she became more and more stressed with every passing day. I had to ask myself: *Why?*

Well, she knew that she had certain prospecting and income levels that I wanted her to hit, and with each new day, she was able to determine with more and more certainty that she was not coming close to hitting that goal. Now, if she had responded to this challenge by changing her typical working day, she might have found a way to work out at our company. But as it stood, she simply kept on doing what she was doing, only with an increasingly desperate look in her eye with every passing day.

About six months down the line, she completely imploded, complaining that the job requirements we had laid out for her were unrealistic, and that her territory was insufficient to sustain her quota goals. (The truth, however, was that the previous salesperson had had no problem meeting quota.)

In fact, the real problem was that she was one of the many salespeople whose stress arises from a permanent feeling of never actually being able to finish anything. If Eleanor had simply buckled down and made the thirty dials a day I had set as a goal for her, I know she would not have had any problem meeting her quota.

We had to let her go. The reason she didn't work out was pretty simple: Faced with a situation that required a new approach, *she stuck with what wasn't working.* If she'd wanted, Eleanor could have taken a much different approach to her day, one far less likely to result in an on-the-job crisis. (See the next chapter.)

Beat Burnout Strategy #12

Group Like Activities Together

Schedule your day strategically.

"Imagination and innovation must drive your efforts every day."

—*Anonymous*

When scheduling your day or setting up your to-do list, do you group together activities that are similar? Do you finish everything in one group before moving on to the next group? Do you do your level best to *keep* similar activities together as you make your way through the day?

I can't tell you the number of salespeople I've worked with who do a little bit of faxing, followed by five minutes of cold calling, followed by an ad hoc meeting with colleagues, followed by a little more faxing . . . That's a recipe for perpetual frustration.

Such salespeople don't set up a schedule for their day, or if they do, they don't follow it. They are, like Eleanor in the previous chapter, prime candidates for problems with burnout-inducing stress.

We have a saying in our office: *The most important appointment you as a salesperson will ever schedule is the one you schedule with yourself.*

What we mean by that is that the responsibility of breaking up specific selling tasks during the day is yours and yours alone.

You must, for instance, make a certain number of prospecting cold calls each and every day. I maintain that your overall stress level—and your likelihood of experiencing burnout—will be much lower if you make a point of scheduling a time for making these calls and then *keep to your schedule,* each and every day. So, if you decide through analysis of your own ratios, that you need twenty dials a day to hit your income targets, it is incumbent upon *you* to schedule perhaps an hour of your day to make these twenty dials. You should do this *each and every business day of the year.*

There are many impressive reasons that you might come across to *avoid* making this kind of commitment and sticking to it. But there is one overwhelming reason to meet your own personal commitments when it comes to time management: You will enjoy your job a whole lot more if you do.

If your typical day follows no set schedule, and if it is largely improvised, this is a sign that you are either: a) postponing essential sales activities that are best not postponed, or b) allowing the day to set the terms for you, rather than the other way around.

The best way out of this stressful career trap is to establish and reinforce a few simple time-management strategies. Establish some kind of daily to-do list. Then group like activities together and assign specific points of the day to each group. For example, set a time for prospecting, administrative work, team meetings, preparing proposals, and so on. Many sales professionals are fond of Palm Pilots and computerized organizers for scheduling these activities, because they can program them to sound an audible alarm when it is time to perform a given task. I take a pragmatic approach—if a tool works for you, use it.

Whatever tool you use, *group all of the like activities together,* and then do your level best to follow your plan. Set up a day that allows you to prospect for a certain period of time, do administrative work for a period of time, send all of your faxes that you gathered during the course of the day at the same time, and have discussions and attend meetings at predetermined times. No, you can't really expect to manage everything down to the minute, and, yes, there will be interruptions. But the strong minded do not wander aimlessly through the day, and every truly successful salesperson I've ever met has been strong minded.

Don't let the day determine your schedule for you. Don't try to "do everything" at various points of the day. Set your priorities and do your best to stick to them. You can never have complete control of the events of your day, of course, but you certainly can *go into your day with a game plan*—and then, at the end of the day, review how close you come to actually sticking to that game plan.

Not everything on your list of possible things to do is as important as everything else. Make conscious *choices* about which people to talk to, which calls to return immediately as opposed to later on, and which proposals to develop as soon as possible. Do not let other people's priorities become your priorities by default.

Beat Burnout Strategy **#13**

Take Back the Morning

How are you starting your day?

"Here comes the sun."

—George Harrison

The period of time *before* you show up at the office can have an immense impact on what you actually accomplish during the course of the day. Is your morning a period of gathering strength—or gathering stress?

Here's an idea. Set your alarm clock for ten minutes earlier than you normally would . . . and spend the time *with yourself* on non-work-related activities. You could use this time sitting and meditating, drinking a cup of tea, reading the paper, or even considering a religious scripture. Whatever you do, make sure it is time devoted to *you and you alone*—in other words, give yourself some time that is not goal oriented or accomplishment oriented.

The Zen Buddhists talk about a kind of attention to the moment that is not involved in "grasping" something out of it. As an experiment, try to give yourself a few such moments every day for the next week. Give yourself a portion of the day where you allow yourself simply to exist, rather than achieve.

It sounds simple, but it can be a remarkably effective stress management technique.

As the day unfolds try to figure out your own natural rhythm. Everyone has a correct working pace, a way of tackling the job that does not make you feel overwhelmed and is not so leisurely as to put you to sleep. Find that balance and do your level best to make it a daily practice—and a part of the schedule you set up for yourself every day.

Beat Burnout Strategy **#14**

Develop a Success Ritual

What's your "recipe" for feeling optimism and energy?

"Successful people develop the habits of doing those things that unsuccessful people choose not to do."

—*Anonymous*

This strategy builds on the previous one of seizing the morning for time alone with yourself. Developing a success ritual of your very own—a set of repeatable actions—can be an extremely effective way to improve your resiliency and your outlook on work (and, indeed, on life). The act of building a repeatable success routine can support you, sustain you, and help you deliver effective responses to the stressful events you will (inevitably) encounter during the course of the day.

So—what *is* a success routine? It's a series of actions *you* choose to do—perhaps upon awakening, but perhaps at points in the day when you feel you need to "recharge." The act of performing this sequence of actions actually changes how you look at the world.

Most effective morning routines, I've noticed, involve some kind of physical action. Some people clap their hands and say,

"Yes!" Some people snap their fingers by their right ear. Some people decide to go out for a quick jog. Some people raise their hands up in the air as if they were at a sporting event, then shake their heads briskly back and forth. Thomas Jefferson used to plunge his feet into ice-cold water.

That cold-water routine, for some people, may be pushing things, although I've heard that some folks still swear by it. Whatever you do, find *some* sort of success ritual that helps to spur a dramatic change in physical and or mental state—a ritual that helps you to recharge your mind and your body. You will find that it helps to perform a *specific* gesture or movement at a time when you are strongly experiencing optimism and energy. Repeating the movement later on will help you to get the feeling back.

Try this: Envision yourself at a period in your life when you felt successful, motivated, and strong. Once you have that image in your mind and are feeling strongly positive, perform your success ritual! The more you do it while you're feeling *good,* the more likely you will be to be able to use the ritual when you're feeling . . . shall we say . . . less than resourceful.

Beat Burnout Strategy **#15**

Make Your Commute Work for You, Not Against You

Our top story: something that will make you feel lousy all morning long.

"There is more to life than increasing its speed."

—Mohandas K. Gandhi, Indian political and religious leader

If you drive to work every morning, you may have found that you've developed a habit of listening to the news in the car on the way into work each day. If this is the case, consider a change of pace.

Try replacing the tales of gloom and doom with a CD of classical music, a comedy recording, or a book on tape. This one simple step can have a dramatic and positive effect on reducing your overall stress level and can help you feel more at home and in control once you do show up at work.

The world will still be there when you get home in the evening. If you insist, you can turn on the latest updates from the Apocalypse at that point!

Beat Burnout Strategy **#16**

Take a Good, Long Look at Your Surroundings

Burnout control begins in the cubicle.

"What a dump!"

—*Bette Davis in the movie* Beyond the Forest *(1949)*

Make sure your work area supports your highest aspirations and increases a sense of comfort. If it does, you'll find that controlling your surroundings will help you control stressful situations—and turn potentially negative experiences into positive ones.

When I say this to salespeople, they sometimes think that I mean that only a Felix Unger–style workspace will do. Not at all! If you are more comfortable having piles of papers around, by all means, have piles of papers around. The point is to make sure that the work environment you step into makes you feel empowered and in control. Can you easily find everything you are looking for? Are there photos of family and friends and loved ones easily visible? Are your next day's tasks set out clearly for you on a list that stays in the same place day after day after day? Is your phone easy to get to?

Does your computer system sync easily and quickly with that of the organization for which you work?

The more "yes" answers you can give to these questions, the more likely you will be able to turn a potentially negative situation into a positive one. Find steps you can take to improve the "feel" of your workplace . . . and you'll improve the likelihood that you'll feel great when you walk in the door to start your working day.

Here's a simple way to do this: Write a note to yourself. There is an old saying that says, "Human beings are not inherently bad, just inherently forgetful." To overcome this problem, take a moment to jot down on a three-by-five card a positive message that will help you keep things in perspective and not lose your focus during the course of the day. For instance, "No one other than me controls my mind, body, and emotions."

Here's another example. It's one of my favorite quotes, and it's on a topic that will never go out of date.

> "A SMILE costs nothing, but gives much. It enriches those who receive, without making poorer those who give. It takes but a moment, but the memory of it sometimes lasts forever. None is so rich or mighty that he can get along without it, and none is so poor but that he can be made rich by it. A smile creates happiness in the home, fosters good will in business, and is the countersign of friendship. It brings rest to the weary, cheer to the discouraged, sunshine to the sad, and is nature's best antidote for trouble. Yet it cannot be bought, begged, borrowed, or stolen, for it is something that is of no value to anyone until it is given away. Some people are too tired to give you a smile. Give them one of yours, as none needs a smile so much as he who has no more to give."
>
> **—Rabbi Samson Raphael Hirsch (1808–88)**

Beat Burnout Strategy **#17**

Go with the Flow

Invoke the opposite of unhealthy stress . . . and get ready to have some fun.

"All serious daring starts from within."

—*Eudora Welty, twentieth-century U.S. writer*

For salespeople (and for lots of other people), the opposite of burnout-inducing stress is called "flow." Even if the term "flow" is unfamiliar to you as you read these words, you know what it is.

If you've ever felt like you were "on your game" . . . If you've ever felt as though you were delivering a presentation that you knew was going to end up in a sale (and you were right!) . . . If you've ever had an initial conversation with a prospect over the phone that you *knew* was going to turn into a first appointment . . . If you've ever reviewed a committee and realized that you were in a perfect position to take advantage of a weakness of one of your competitors, and then executed on that opportunity . . . Then you already know what "flow" is.

The flow is a sense of effortless, attentive, productive, nonanxiety-producing work. It's work you conduct for yourself and for whatever you're focusing on. Not for other people. Not for your sales manager. Not for the competition. And not for anyone you're afraid might say no. When you're in the flow, you're working for yourself.

My favorite example of somebody who's working in the flow comes from an older salesperson whose strategies have been an inspiration to me for many years. It was my privilege to accompany him on a visit, where he encountered some resistance from his prospect.

A less experienced salesperson—me, for instance—would have reacted defensively to the prospect's stiff body language, unresponsive answers to questions, and brisk dismissals. When my mentor, whom I'll call Charlie, tried to progress to the next phase of the relationship by scheduling another meeting, he got nowhere. I watched Charlie with great interest. What would he do now?

I knew exactly how *I* would respond to the challenge Charlie faced: It had happened to me many times before. I had frozen up and started reciting something: my product brochure, or the reasons I knew my company was better than the competition, or the many advantages the prospect would experience as a result of working with me. When we feel stress—in the form of resistance from a prospect, say—we are likely to react by falling back on what we are already familiar with. So when *I* faced a prospect shutting down on me, I fell back on what I was familiar with. I made familiar canned speeches and hoped for the best.

To my surprise, that's not what Charlie did.

What Charlie did was something very different. He looked the prospect in the eye with an air of genuine concern, put down the notepad and pen that he'd been using to take notes and illustrate his points, and said, in all sincerity, "Mr. Jones, I can tell that there's a problem here. Usually, by this point in my initial meeting with someone, the person I'm talking to has decided to meet with me again. And you just told me a moment ago that you weren't ready to make any commitment like that. Well, Mr. Jones, if that's really how you feel about it, after all that I showed you about our service, and after what I've been able to deliver to literally hundreds of people in your industry, then I know for sure that the problem isn't with our service, but it's with the way I've described it. For you to tell me you have absolutely no interest whatsoever, I must have done something terribly wrong in delivering my presentation today. So, would you please tell me what it was and where I went wrong?"

What he said was not accusing. It wasn't tense. It wasn't dry recitation of facts and figures. To the contrary, Charlie seemed spontaneous and relaxed and engaged and connected to the other person—just what I certainly would not have been in a similar situation. He was able to ask that question honestly, because he really truly did believe that the service he offered was superior to any others that were available on the market, and he really believed that the prospect to whom he was speaking had genuine application for that service.

I watched in amazement as the prospect's body language and focus shifted dramatically. Charlie said nothing. I certainly said nothing. The prospect straightened up in his chair, took another look at what Charlie had been sketching on the pad, and then said words that I'll remember for the rest of my life.

"Charlie," he said, "the problem isn't with you, it's all on my end. We've got a budget freeze and as much as I'd like to be able to use you, I wouldn't be able to do that until at least three months from now."

Charlie began taking notes again and within twenty minutes he had closed the sale based on an arrangement whereby the prospect would not be invoiced for our services until the beginning of the next quarter. As we walked out of the building, I shook my head and told Charlie how deeply I had been impressed by what he had done in that office. To my surprise, he did not really know what I was talking about. I explained that I was impressed by the "maneuver" of assuming full responsibility for the sale had allowed him to turn a rejection into an order.

He looked at me a little oddly and then shook his head. "That wasn't a maneuver," he told me. "That was the truth. That's just what you do if you really can't figure out why the person wouldn't be buying. You ask where you went wrong."

Charlie's effortless rescue of that sale can probably be replicated in 100 different ways, but the most important thing to bear in mind is that *it won't work if you're tense.* You have to be in the flow for it to work. Working in the flow does not mean using high pressure selling tactics. It means knowing what you're doing and not being afraid of what may happen next. During that meeting, Charlie was in the flow. You can be in the flow, too. And you can apply this "in the flow" feeling to virtually any phase of the relationship with a prospect. You just have to be willing to tell the truth.

Let me give you an example of what I mean. When I am cold-calling prospects on the telephone, as I still do, I will frequently hear the person on the other end of the line say something like this,

"Steve, I just have absolutely no interest whatsoever in talking to you about this."

Now, I have heard that response approximately 500,000 times over the years. So it would be odd if I dealt with that response in a panicked or anxious way. Either I *am* going to be able to turn that objection around or I am *not.* There are only one or two outcomes to consider, and either one is fine with me. If I can turn the response around, I can schedule an appointment with the person—the odds are pretty good on that. If I *cannot* turn it around, I am simply going to go on to the next call.

So here is what I say: "You know, Mr. Smith, that is really interesting—because that is exactly what ABC Company told me at first when I called them. Right now, they are one of our best customers. Just out of curiosity, have you ever done any sales training before?"

I'm in the flow!

With that simple turnaround, which I have executed in various forms countless times, I take the energy out of the person's objection, redirect the conversation, reduce the stress of the exchange, and enter my own flow. I am controlling the conversation because I am controlling the response the other person can give me. As a result of what I've just said, we now are talking about what kind of sales training the other person has done. If I get a response directly related to that, then I'm in great shape. If not, I thank the person for his or her time and move on. I have done this so many times and have become so comfortable with the exchange that when I make calls, it is not a stressful experience at all. I've got the right process, and it is simply a matter of executing it.

When you are in the flow, you do not have to worry about what comes next. You are simply executing something that you have done so many times, that you realize there really is nothing to worry about. It's a little bit like driving a car down a long highway in the middle of the night. You've been driving for many miles for hours and hours on end and suddenly there is a new stimulus in the corner of your eye. A familiar exit, one that you know you are supposed to take. If you've been down that highway many times, you won't know exactly *when* that exit will show up, but you will know that it *is* eventually going to show up—and when it does, it will be of no particular surprise. The act of slowing, getting in the right lane, setting your turn signal, and so on won't be stressful activities for you. They'll simply be part of a comfortable transition from one activity to the next.

That same open-ended, confident mind-set is exactly what good salespeople have when they rely on strategies they've practiced many, many, many times. And that's the key to getting in the flow: practice.

In my experience, in order to get the flow to work for you, you really must be quite serious about drilling various sales strategies over and over and over again. You must drill something that works for you—like the turnaround to a familiar objection—until it becomes as familiar to you as your own name.

Beat Burnout Strategy #18

Ask Your Manager for Help

Remember: You're not in this alone.

"Beware, as long as you live, of judging people by appearances."

—Jean de la Fontaine, seventeenth-century French poet

It never ceases to amaze me how many salespeople and managers seem to believe that selling is something that should involve only salespeople. We have a proud tradition at my company of involving managers in the sales process. Managers can help to move the sales process forward in any number of ways; any event involving a prospect or customer that causes you to feel stressed may be worth discussing with your manager.

Consider, for instance, the common, stressful situation where the prospect is unable to "get off the fence." You can't get any feedback one way or another, and you suspect (but can't confirm) that the prospect may be talking to other vendors. Rather than sit there and stew about your indecisive customer, or (even worse) project the income on your next quarterly activity report, *ask your manager for help*. He or she can quickly resolve exactly what is happening in the relationship simply by placing a phone call. The manager can open a conversation by saying something like, "I understand we're going to be doing business together."

Talk about *constructive* stress!

If what the manager has just said to your prospect is true—if there is a real chance of doing business with this person in the near term—then the true state of affairs will instantly become clear. The contact will immediately agree to what the manager has said, and will say something like: "You know, I think you're right. I think we will be doing something with your company."

If, on the other hand, there is still some kind of obstacle to your working together, you may rest assured that the contact will identify what that obstacle is for your sales manager! The prospect will say something like this: "What? Doing business together? Well, that may be a little premature. You see, the thing is . . ."

In either event, the advantage is yours. You will either accelerate action and commitment (or uncover information that you wouldn't have been able to uncover on your own) . . . or you'll quickly identify the reasons that your contact is *unlikely* to buy from you, thereby keeping you from investing any more time in that relationship.

Managers and supervisors have a great way of getting to the bottom of things for salespeople. They also know what you're up against. Talk to your manager about what's happening in your world! Tell him or her what's up with each of your prospects . . . and ask for help!

Beat Burnout Strategy **#19**

Find Another Point of Entry

Work with your manager to identify other potential allies within your target organization.

> "Enter a house by the right door."
>
> —*Traditional saying*

Sometimes burnout-inducing stress arises because we spend all our time with a particular contact within the target company . . . and we get nowhere.

If the relationship with your contact is not working out, and you're not gathering any meaningful information or securing any next steps, *try to find another point of entry.* Again, you can always ask your supervisor for help in brainstorming or in developing a new channel. Sometimes the simplest approaches are the ones that are most likely to turn a burnout-inducing stress situation into a constructive stress situation.

When one of my salespeople tells me that he or she is having no luck moving forward in a relationship with a particular person in the target company, I usually call that contact's number at a time when I know I'm likely to reach his or her voicemail system, and

I'll say something like this: "Hi, this is Steve Schiffman, president of D.E.I. Management Group; I'm calling regarding John Smith." That is the whole message that I leave.

When the person calls me back, which he or she inevitably will, the dynamic of the call is a lot more favorable than if I had called the person and interrupted him or her in the middle of something. After exchanging a few pleasantries, I will say something along the following lines: "You know, I called because I was talking to John Smith about the last meeting he had with you. He told me it did not go well, and I wanted to apologize and find out exactly what the problem is."

Inevitably the contact will explain that the problem really was not the salesperson, but something else that is going on within the organization. My next step at that phase usually is to find a way to schedule a meeting between me, the salesperson, the salesperson's contact, and someone new within the target organization—someone who *can* help us to move the sale forward. By approaching the contact and offering an apology, I've changed the entire dynamic of the relationship.

Beat Burnout Strategy #20

Escape the "Rejection Trap"

Understand what "no" really means.

> "Patience is the companion of wisdom."
>
> —*St. Augustine (345–430)*

We come now to a place many salespeople consider to be the most fearsome territory of all: the dreaded Land of No. Many salespeople cite rejection as a primary reason for feeling stress and a contributing factor to feeling disenchantment about the job. It is entirely possible that rejection is a major cause of burnout in a sales position. Here, perhaps, is the most important area for us to implement the principle of not *consciously* embracing burnout-inducing stress.

But what *is* rejection?

Just about anyone who spends any time developing a sales plan and implementing it over time comes to realize that "rejection" is just another way of saying "statistical process." If you're a salesperson, taking rejection personally is a little like taking the weather personally. I call the mistake of taking rejection personally "falling into the rejection trap."

Let me illustrate what I mean by posing a practical question. If your goal is to set fifteen new first appointments over the next three weeks, and you are willing to make the effort to reach out to total strangers to set those appointments, what do you think will happen on the way to achieving that goal?

It should go without saying that you will *not* call fifteen people and schedule fifteen appointments. En route to those fifteen appointments, you will inevitably run into some people who tell you they *do not* want to meet with you. It is simple delusion to assume that accomplishing any worthwhile sales goal—such as getting those fifteen appointments—can be achieved at a one-to-one ratio. You are never, ever going to call fifteen people and schedule fifteen appointments. Period.

By the same token, let's say you hit your goal, and you *do* schedule those fifteen first appointments. What happens then? Well, if you've been selling for more than about ten minutes, you already know that you should not expect to turn all fifteen of those first appointments into fifteen active prospects. (An "active prospect" is someone who continues to agree to talk about buying from you by scheduling a second meeting.) And guess what? You are never going to take those fifteen first appointments and turn them into fifteen perfect proposals, either.

No matter how well you execute your sales process, you're simply never going to avoid encountering people who tell you, "No thank you." Discussions with such people are basically written into your job description.

Now, to me, that's not really "rejection." I save words like "rejection" for situations where someone is, say, turning down a proposal of marriage. A person saying "no, thanks, I'm not ready to buy from you today" is more of a benign statistical inevitability. It's a sign that I'm doing something right—namely, talking to enough prospects to generate the "no" responses that make "yes" responses possible. Labeling that outcome with the emotionally loaded term "rejection" doesn't help me or support me, so I don't do it.

Don't choose terminology that makes it easy for you to create feelings of frustration and unhealthy stress in your daily routine. In other words, don't fall into the "rejection trap"! Choose smarter words than "rejection" to describe both for yourself and others the experience you're having. Don't go looking for ways to take that experience personally!

Instead . . . *count the numbers!* Find out *how many* "no" answers it typically takes you to generate one appointment. Find out *how many* appointments it typically takes you to generate one prospect. Find out *how many* prospects it typically takes you to generate one sale. Once you start looking at "no" answers as part of a statistical process, and start taking control of your own internal vocabulary, you'll be in control of your own emotions . . . and your own career.

Beat Burnout Strategy **#21**

Understand Your Own Numbers

Know why you do what you do.

"The journey of a thousand miles begins with a single step."

—Lao Tzu (c. 570–490 B.C.), founder of Taoism

People are fond of saying that sales is a numbers game. As I have said many times, it is more accurate to believe that sales is a ratios game . . . a much more helpful idea when it comes to maintaining control over your day, your week, your quarter, and your career. Feeling in control is an important weapon for beating burnout.

Let me explain exactly what I mean. Every day that I'm not training, I dial the phone fifteen times. My aim is to speak to seven decision-makers and to set one appointment for a new face-to-face meeting. I always ask our sales training participants a question about this habit of mine: "*Why* do I make those fifteen dials a day?"

I've asked that question thousands of times. People have told me I make those dials in order to gain an advantage over my competition, or to secure my position as a leading sales trainer, or to reach out to new customers and build rapport with them, or for a dozen other reasons. In fact, the reason I make fifteen dials a day is because that's what it takes for me to close a certain number of sales. In my case, the number fifteen links up to one new sale a week.

Watch how it works. I know that if I set an appointment every single solitary day, I will have five new appointments each week. If I add that to the three additional visits I typically make as follow-up meetings, I have eight face-to-face meetings on the average week. That number—eight—is an important one for me, because it happens to correspond precisely with my closing ratio. I know, as a statistical fact, that for every eight face-to-face meetings I go on, I will close one new sale. So eight visits in one week equals, on average, one closed sale.

When I tell you that I pick up the phone fifteen times a day, and that each time I pick it up I dial a brand new person, what I'm really telling you is that I am *supporting my own income goal* of closing one new sale a week, or fifty new pieces of business each and every year. So the answer to the question, "Why does Steve make the fifteen dials every day?" is pretty simple: I need to make fifteen calls a day to create fifty new pieces of business. In other words, I know what works for me statistically.

Sometimes I'll ask a salesperson, "How many cold calls did you make yesterday?" The person will look at me for a minute and say, "Uh. Twelve." Then I'll say, "Great—why that number?" Silence.

Most salespeople *do not connect their daily activity numbers to their quarterly or yearly quota numbers.* They have no idea how things hook up, how what they do today affects the money they earn a month from now. And that, in my experience, is a why salespeople eventually experience burnout.

Monitor your own daily numbers! Set your own daily activity targets in accordance with your income goals! Specifically, keep track of your dials, completed calls (that is, conversations with decision-makers), first appointments set, total visits (including follow-up visits), and closed sales. Monitor these ratios closely. Doing so will tell you where you need to improve your selling skills.

As a practical matter, I've found that the only way to pull this off is to make record keeping something of an obsession. But the effort is worth it. It is no coincidence that the salespeople who have the biggest problem dealing with the emotional effects of rejection are, in my experience, the very same salespeople who refuse to set daily performance targets and monitor their actual activity toward those targets. Such salespeople assume that *some force other than their own actions* is guiding their performance. This is a huge—and usually quite stressful—mistake!

If, after, say, a month's worth of calls, you have monitored exactly what activities you undertook and what positive sales results you achieved, you will be in a position to understand exactly what you're going to earn this quarter . . . and exactly what you need to do to improve your income performance to the level that makes sense for you.

You will be in control of your numbers, your career, and (most important of all) your own mind-set.

Beat Burnout Strategy **#22**

Abolish the Sales Slump

Learn how to put an end to the number-one cause of burnout-inducing stress—the self-imposed sales slump.

"Do all the good you can, by all the means you can, in all the ways you can, as long as ever you can."

—John Wesley, eighteenth-century founder of the Methodist Church

---

Have you ever experienced a down curve or slump in your sales? You know the experience I'm talking about. All of a sudden you realize that you're behind quota, and it dawns on you that you're going have to work like crazy to catch up. That adrenaline-pumping, "oh my gosh I just realized I'm behind quota" phenomenon is not only common, it's exhausting after a while! It may well be the single most traumatizing experience a salesperson has to deal with; it is certainly a major contributor to burnout-inducing stress. This phenomenon, in my experience, tends to happen over and over again to the same salespeople. It is a result, not of bad luck or a lousy territory or any of the other reasons people imagine, but of *not prospecting for new business on a regular basis.*

How does it happen? Let's say that, right now, you have twenty prospects—and by prospects I mean people who are currently in discussions with you about buying what you have to sell—who are willing to set aside a portion of their calendar for a meeting or discussion with you. So, you have twenty prospects and you make one sale. How many prospects do you have left?

Well, let's assume you close one out of every five of your prospects. (That's a pretty realistic ratio.) This means every time you make a sale, you lose five prospects. One closes, but four go away—they do not buy from you for whatever reason. What this means is that your closing ratio dictates that you need many more active prospects at any given time than the total number of sales you expect your prospect base to deliver. It only makes sense, right?

Look at it again. You have twenty prospects and you close a single sale. And you do not add any new prospects to your prospect base. How many prospects should you *really* assume that you have? The answer is fifteen, even though it may look for a moment as though you have twenty. And the failure to recognize that the right answer is fifteen, not twenty, is what puts so many salespeople through the stressful "peaks and valleys" cycle over and over again. The chart on the next page shows how it looks.

The prospects that you meet with *drop out over time* . . . but you can be certain they in fact *will* drop out. What's more, they will drop out in accordance with *your own closing ratios.* So if you make a second sale, you will be down to *ten* real prospects. Get it? And if you make yet another sale without replenishing your prospect base, you will be down to *five* prospects. And then after the next sale you will go down to *zero* prospects and you will have to start the process all over again.

Around my office we have a common saying about sales: "Whenever you close a sale, you didn't just lose your best prospect . . . you lost five of your best prospects." Now, how do you make that stress-producing cycle a thing of the past? Read on.

Peaks and valleys cycle

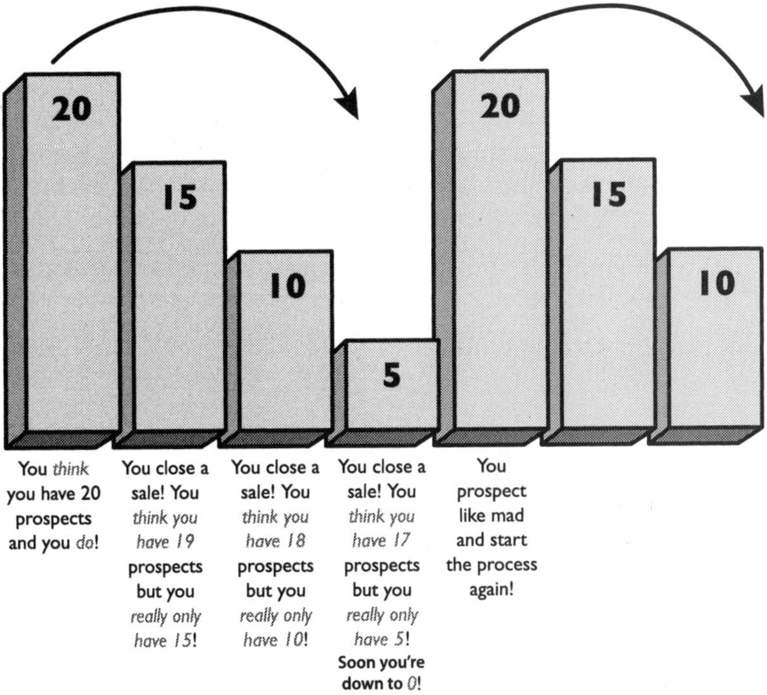

20

15

10

5

20

15

10

You *think* you have 20 prospects and you *do*!

You close a sale! You *think you have 19* prospects but you *really only have 15*!

You close a sale! You *think you have 18* prospects but you *really only have 10*!

You close a sale! You *think you have 17* prospects but you *really only have 5*! Soon you're down to *0*!

You prospect like mad and start the process again!

Beat Burnout Strategy **#23**

Learn the Ten Commandments for Making Sales Slumps a Thing of the Past

The secrets of maintaining a steady base of prospects.

"In order to be successful in sales, you have to see enough people, they must be the right kind of people, you have to tell them your story, and you have to do it every day."

—*H. Jackson Brown Jr.,* New York Times *bestselling author*

Here's a guarantee. If you faithfully follow all ten of the following commandments for managing and sustaining your prospect base, then the dreaded "peaks-and-valleys syndrome" will never again threaten to ruin your quarter, deplete your bank account, or make you wish you did something else for a living. Talk about an antidote to unhealthy stress!

Here are the ten commandments.

I. **Set the goal for the number of first appointments you want to maintain at all times.** Learn your conversion ratios. Find out how many first appointments you need every week to support your quarterly or monthly income goals. Make the adjustments that make sense for you to achieve your goals.

II. **Make cold calls daily with the objective of setting at least one new appointment every day.** This does not include networking meetings. Block the time out and cold-call for an *uninterrupted* period. Don't send e-mail or receive incoming calls during that block of time. Approach this activity with discipline and a sense of urgency.

III. **Track your dials, completed calls, and appointments set on a daily basis.** Compile your results daily; benchmark your activity to assess your success and help determine your ratios.

IV. **Do not stop dialing if you are not meeting with success.** Stand up, take a break, practice, read this book—do whatever you have to do, but *don't stop.* If you are calling within a particular industry and are finding appointment-making tough, diversify your leads. Hit your daily target, no matter what.

V. **Always be prepared to cold-call.** Have an organized, identified lead list ready with you always, and use it when you have unexpected time available. Do not research or prioritize your calls between calls—this is your peak sales time! Do your organizing work off-peak.

VI. **Learn the appropriate third-party references.** Use your company's past and current success stories—but *don't* let a lack of complete knowledge deter your efforts. As you improve, you will learn that being able to memorize the specifics of success stories really doesn't matter that much anyway.

VII. **Practice your cold calling process until you are comfortable and confident with your approach.** Practice your turnarounds until they're second nature. (To develop effective phone turnarounds, see my book *Cold Calling Techniques (That Really Work!),* and also refer to commandment X.)

VIII. **Tape record your side of your calls.** Do this on a frequent basis and review them to make continuous improvements in your pitch, tone, dynamics, style, and smoothness.

IX. **Don't kid yourself.** Sales come from prospects and prospects come from appointments.

X. **Contact us.** E-mail *contactus@dei-sales.com* and ask for the *free* e-learning course, *Sixteen Keys to Getting More Appointments.* We'll send you some easy-to-implement ideas on securing new appointments by phone. (Be sure to mention the course by name, and to specify that you heard about it by reading this book.)

Beat Burnout Strategy #24

Take Twenty-One Days at a Time

What habit for beating burnout are you trying to program yourself to follow?

"Stress is an ignorant state.
It believes that everything is an emergency."

—Natalie Goldberg, American author

As a salesperson, you can develop many simple little habits to help reduce the chances of feeling burned out. But the tricky thing is, it takes about twenty-one days of consistent effort to replace a bad habit (or no habit at all) with a good one.

Not long ago, one of our employees on a coast-to-coast flight suddenly heard a strange noise from across the aisle. He looked over and immediately noticed that the man in the seat across from him was choking on a piece of meat. At the same moment, a flight attendant appeared, unbuckled the choking passenger, whipped him around, stood over him, and expertly administered the Heimlich maneuver. In a matter of seconds, the meat that had been stuck in this man's throat was successfully expelled, and a life-threatening incident had been averted.

After that event, our employee asked the flight attendant how on earth she had managed to spot the choking passenger and take action so quickly. The answer was a surprising one: "People choking on planes is one of the most common reasons for airborne deaths, and it's a major area of liability for the airline. So during our training, we are drilled repeatedly in administering the Heimlich maneuver. We get pretty good at it. They make us practice it over and over again."

Our employee was still curious about the matter, however, so he continued by asking, "When you say over and over again, what do you mean?"

"How many times would you guess?" asked the flight attendant, a smile on her face.

"Twenty or thirty," said our employee.

"Try between nine hundred fifty and one thousand," said the flight attendant.

Now, you might think that having to drill a particular procedure 950 times is a bit excessive. But think about it from the airline's point of view. The potential risk—a dead passenger on a transcontinental flight—is certainly worth the effort of practicing the Heimlich maneuver that many times. And certainly the passenger whose life was saved and his family would probably object to any planned reduction in the number of practice sessions!

The most potentially useful habits must be reinforced, not simply a few times, but many, many times—so many times that the action in question becomes instantly habitual during a moment of stress. Sales, as we have seen is full of stressful situations: People say strange things to you on the phone, people turn down proposals you have put a great deal of work into, people react oddly and unpredictably during face-to-face interviews.

Now, as I've mentioned, it is a law of human nature that we respond to stressful situations by falling back on that which we already know well. So, if what you know best is talking about your products, then, when you find yourself in a stressful situation, such as a meeting with a total stranger, you are very likely to fall back on that which you regard, perhaps subconsciously, as the "safest" course of action—that which you have done many, many, many times, namely, talking about your product.

Consider again the example of the flight attendant. In a life-threatening emergency, we do not want that flight attendant to have to stop and think about what steps to carry out, or to fall back on a panic response, such as screaming and shouting or asking someone else for help. Instead, we want that flight attendant to be able to respond instantly and effectively! The same is true of sales. We want to avoid making a stressful situation more stressful, and the best way to do that is to drill good sales habits so many times that they appear instantly during stressful situations.

It is important for us as salespeople to *consciously develop* certain *constructive responses,* because they protect against the possibility of frustration and eventual sales burnout. We tend to fall back on that with which we are most familiar, so if we develop constructive responses, and use them regularly in sales situations, we will naturally fall back on them in times of stress. If we use *unconstructive responses* to stressful situations, and use them on a fairly regular basis, the simple fact that we repeat those unconstructive responses time and time again is enough to solidify them!

I don't care who you are, I don't care what level of proficiency you've developed as a salesperson, and I don't care what your income level is (or was). *There is some kind of better selling habit you could be instilling.* My experience is that "implanting" a constructive selling habit—one that can help you turn a burnout-inducing stress situation into a creative stress situation—takes about twenty-one calendar days of consistent effort and thought. (I'm not saying that you need twenty-one solid days of work on nothing else *but* instilling the habit, but I am saying you should think about how to implement it, and try to do so at least once a day, for twenty-one days.)

What are the bad habits we are likely to have *now* that make it easier for burnout to take root? You will find such a list of negative habits in Part Two of this book—as well as advice for turning them around and instilling the appropriate positive habits in their place!

Part Two

Beating the Habits That Make Long-Term Burnout Possible

In this part of the book, you learn about the most common habits that lead to burnout—and how to overcome them.

Burnout Habit **#1**

Selling Yourself a Bill of Goods

Master the neglected art of telling yourself the truth about the situation you face.

> "Never B.S. yourself."
>
> —*Anonymous*

Instead, make a habit of being honest with yourself. You may be the only one you can count on to tell the truth about the situation you face! To beat burnout, we have to be honest with ourselves about what we are really facing, and what resources we can bring to bear in dealing with the situation we face. To beat burnout, we should make a habit of being brutally frank with ourselves.

This can be tricky for two reasons. First salespeople have a certain responsibility to instill optimism in their work—it's part of the job description—yet being optimistic sometimes results in our overlooking important real-world elements of our situation. Second, to improve our image in these politically correct times, as sales professionals we have become more in tune with our prospects and have developed more honest relationships with our customers (certainly a welcome development!), but we must be more honest where it perhaps counts the most—with ourselves. A significant number of burnout cases in sales, I believe, come from situations where salespeople have "sold themselves a bill of goods"—and perpetuated some common, seductive, and fatally misconceived ideas about sales.

The following are just a few examples of the most common sales lies that I've seen salespeople use on themselves. These lies, which I believe are associated with burnout-inducing stress, can actually inhibit success, prevent salespeople from achieving both short-term and long-term sales goals, and increase the likelihood that they will find themselves standing on an unsteady ledge of denial that will eventually crumble beneath them.

Lie #1: Someday I will not need to prospect.

Some salespeople look at apparently "successful" sales professionals and believe that once they cultivate a few big accounts, they will never have to prospect for new business again. This is among the most dangerous sales lies. Without a steady stream of new prospects, a salesperson is putting his or her income stream in jeopardy. All that has to happen is the loss of one major account, and then the salesperson is back to square one. It's important for you to prospect regularly to protect your income base so that you're not reliant for success on the unpredictability of one or several major existing accounts.

Lie #2: It's OK to lie—just a little.

Not really. Lies have an interesting way of catching up with you. Whether you're lying to your manager, coworker, or prospects, you will find it's really much better to tell the truth—even if you risk losing an account. Your reputation and credibility is the key to your success. Be truthful with everyone, even on minor issues. If you do that, people will find it easy to trust you on big issues.

Lie #3: Prospects really need our product or service.

Whatever you sell—cars, computer systems, insurance, engineering services—you should understand that nobody really "needs" you. Prospects have been using or doing something else without you, and they can continue doing that or something else indefinitely. If they needed you, they would have called you! Your job is to *challenge and make a persuasive case to change* the status quo, not to assume that it is working in your favor. It isn't!

When you call someone you've never spoken to before, you must understand that you're the very last individual that person was hoping to talk to when he or she picked up the phone. What you say must be so exciting, so compelling, delivered with such conviction, and associated with so much enthusiasm, that the other person is willing to stop what he or she is doing and *listen* to why it makes sense to re-evaluate everything the person ever thought about his or her "needs." You can do that, in my experience, only by focusing on what the person *does.*

So, what do you offer your prospects as a means to help them do what they are doing—better? Consider the person you think "needs" a computer. He or she can dictate a letter, write it out manually, or hire an outside service to compose it. What you offer is not something that "uncovers a need" or "spotlights the pain"—but something that will help him or her to get the job done *more efficiently*. That's the best way to position what you offer. That's what you have to try to focus the other person's attention on. Trying to build your selling routine around any other principle—pain, need, problem, or any other label you choose—is to sentence yourself to a seemingly endless series of pointless battles and squabbles with prospects and leads . . . squabbles that really won't yield very much in the way of meaningful information. That's a recipe for burnout-inducing stress.

Lie #4: "It's business—I never take it personally."

This is true only for salespeople who happen to be saints. If a prospect stands you up, it does hurt you—personally. When you've put hours upon hours into a presentation, and the sale doesn't close, that also hurts you personally. The fact is that selling is part of your life. It's your livelihood. When a setback happens, the only thing worse than overemphasizing the personal aspect of the experience is denying that it's happened in the first place. That's denial, and it's not a good way to approach your job. Accept whatever took place and deal with the blow emotionally. Pretending it doesn't hurt is likely to lead to increased stress levels and a higher chance of job burnout.

Lie #5: "Don't worry about the competition—they'll never reach us," or "We really don't have any meaningful competitors."

This sales lie has caused great financial damage for major corporations such as GM and IBM. Even if you are in a high-tech field selling a breakthrough product or service, you have got to realize someone else is selling, or is about to sell, a product or service that could make your product obsolete. Read your customer's industry publications, and yours, regularly. Always seek out information on your existing competition, as well as products that can be used in place of your product. Don't kid yourself! The competition is usually a lot closer to you than you think. That's the nature of our free enterprise system. "Always assume your competitors are smarter than you are," wrote Shailesh Mehta, President and CEO of Granite Hill Capital Ventures, and former chairman of the board and CEO of Providian Financial Corporation, an S&P 500 company. It's sound advice.

Lie #6: "People will be more likely to buy from me if they fail to show up for an initial appointment—because they will feel that they owe me."

The fault with this lie is that it overlooks the inconvenient fact that prospects don't really owe you anything. You are going after prospects for the sale, and whether or not they feel (momentarily) guilty or not for missing an appointment, forgetting to return your call, or committing any other social gaffe, *that feeling will not affect their buying decisions.* (Would a mistake in etiquette persuade you to buy, say, a new car from a salesperson representing a model that didn't really make sense for you?) Apply your sales skills to the fullest, no matter what you feel your prospect may or may not owe you. Maybe, if you're lucky, he or she plans on being polite to you after the sale. But that doesn't mean you have the sale in your hand!

Lie #7: "Sales are really easy to make here."

Complacency is among the most dangerous sales traps, and among the most common causes of job dissatisfaction. When sales close easily, it's dangerous to sit back and imagine they will always close easily. The "easy sale" could have been a fluke, or it could have been more complex than you imagine. We often don't know what actually goes into a buying decision. Either way, taking customers for granted is a big mistake.

Lie #8: "This prospect is a sure thing."

Unfortunately, no prospect is a sure thing. Even after a contract is signed, a sale can still fall through. Use meaningful criteria to identify the real "sure things"—such as "freight on dock" for products, or "date of service scheduled" for services. (Some years ago I came up with a tongue-in-cheek rule for identifying the viability of sales prospects: "The prospect you are most likely to consider a 'sure thing' is the one most likely to fall out of your prospect base.")

Lie #9: "Your success is all that matters to me, Ms. Prospect. If you succeed—then I succeed."

This lie, when spoken by salespeople during the vendor selection process, is usually a rationalization for sitting back and letting the competition, or people within the client's organization, take control of your sales process! Your goal should be to make sure both you and the client succeed *as you've planned* to succeed. If your prospect is looking into competitors' services and pricing, you should know about that and get involved. If your account has been "handed over" to technical support people, you should find a way to stay involved in the relationship.

Make no mistake: A sales career is hard work, and it carries with it a fair number of ups and downs. There's no reason to add to the number of "down" experiences by misleading yourself and leaving yourself open to many more rude awakenings. Don't B.S. yourself. A sales career can be the most emotionally and financially rewarding career of all the choices open to you—if you make a habit of leveling with yourself. It is crucial to be truthful with yourself as well as your prospects so you can achieve the career results you desire based upon hard work, trust, and solid relationships that benefit both parties.

And let's face it—if you don't give yourself the straight story, you may not be able to get it from anyone else!

Burnout Habit #2

Setting Uninspiring Goals

Choose a goal that jazzes you!

> "The struggle is to do one's best, to keep the brain and conscience clear, [and] never to be swayed by unworthy motives."
>
> —*Dwight D. Eisenhower*

Most of the highly stressed salespeople I've run into have short-term goals that sound like this: "Close such-and-such a deal." "Get my boss off my back." "Avoid missing quota again this quarter."

These are uninspiring goals. They're not the kinds of goals that get you excited, and they're certainly not the kinds of goals that inspire you to demand the best from yourself. People who consistently move toward worthy goals, set their sights higher than before, and regularly demand new levels of performance from themselves are, in my experience, highly unlikely to suffer from professional burnout!

If a goal does not *energize* you automatically, guess what? It's not a good goal! Those salespeople who work for a purpose, who have a sense of mission, who know exactly where they're going and why, are the ones who are best positioned to transform potentially debilitating stress into creative stress. Those goals sound like this:

"Take my wife [husband] on a cruise ship to Hawaii." "Put a shiny red vintage Thunderbird in perfect condition in my parking space each morning." "Make enough money to be able to give $10,000 to the American Cancer Society." Those are goals that can get you up early in the morning!

Some people really are strongly motivated by money. You can certainly set your goals in terms of a dollar figure; just be sure to do so in a positive sense. Such a positive goal might sound like this: "Reach the president's club and secure commission income of more than $100,000." If this kind of goal excites you—and for some very competitive people such a goal is indeed highly motivating—you should be ready to roll. Just be sure to state your goal *in the positive.* (Don't, for instance, state your goal in the negative: "Avoid missing out again on making the president's club." This kind of goal will send your brain a series of negative messages whenever you review it.) I do want to emphasize, though, that many people *enjoy* financial rewards but are not strongly *motivated* by them. If this is the case for you, you might want to find a way to connect your financial goals to a tangible, physical goal such as a car, a vacation, or some other reward.

You probably already know that you're supposed to commit your goal to a clear, written form and post it someplace where you can see it during the course of the day. If you are not already doing this, I can only assume that's because you've either lost sight of an important element of long-term career success, or you simply haven't heard of the dramatic income difference that relates to committing goals to paper. There was a famous study done some years ago that tracked alumni from a prestigious university. Those members who made a habit of committing their goals to paper, and were still following through on that habit in the years after graduation, had an average net worth that *exceeded that of all the other alumni combined.*

Junk the demotivating goal. Set the right goal, the one that really jazzes you. Write it down and post it someplace where you can see it. Review your goal regularly, say every three months. Revise it when appropriate.

Burnout Habit **#3**

Not Tracking Your Own Time

What, specifically, did you do yesterday—and how much of what you did brought you closer to your goals?

"Let us not look back in anger or forward in fear, but around in awareness."

—James Thurber (1894–1961), American humorist

Effective time management skills make all the difference. If you develop them, you can keep your life in balance. If you don't, you will constantly feel stressed, behind schedule, and (probably) sleep deprived. That last problem is particularly serious, since no salesperson who is a victim of constant insomnia is likely to perform well at work.

Poor time management is much more common than effective time management. My experience is that a failure to closely and carefully track one's own time *as it is actually spent* is a major obstacle to diagnosing specific time-management problems. So one of the steps I recommend to any salesperson who is feeling cynical about his or her profession, or about sales work in general, is to evaluate a working day very closely and then make a radical and conscious series of changes in the next daily schedule.

I recommend this step because of my belief in a principle that I consider a "golden rule": *"Obsession without evaluation of habits results in chaos."* Chaos produces a supremely negative, stressful outcome in sales—or in any other line of work, for that matter. Chaos is, I think, a common element of the later stages of sales burnout, and it is attributable, ultimately, to poor time-management techniques.

When we feel that we have no sense of control over our day—when we have no clear indication of cause and effect, of how one thing we do positively affects an outcome in another area—then we are the victims of chaos. When we seem to be driven by circumstances rather than driving them, we are the victims of chaos. When our daily schedule never allows us any time to evaluate exactly what the daily activities actually led to, then we are the victims of chaos.

So, what do you do to avoid chaos? *Evaluate your habits.* Find out what outcomes those habits are *actually delivering* for you. Are they taking you closer to your goal, or moving you further away from it?

Identify a particular sales-related goal, one that's important to you and that you're willing to work hard to attain. (For instance, you might choose the goal of closing six new sales this month so that you can take your spouse on a vacation to the tropics.) Now take a brand-new notebook and keep track, for one full day, of *everything* you do on the job. Write it all down. Use fifteen-minute increments and list the most important thing you did during that time period.

At the end of the day—take a look at your time log. Put a plus sign by activities that ended up moving you *closer* to your goal. Put a circle by activities that had *no effect* on whether you moved closer to your goal. Put a minus sign by activities that actually ended up moving you *away* from your goal. Now ask yourself these questions:

- How does what you learn about your day—about what's working and what's not—affect your priorities for tomorrow?
- How many different things did you do during the day?
- When did you do them?
- How much time did you allocate to each task?
- Were there ever times when you were "busying" yourself with activities that had *no effect whatsoever* on whether you moved forward toward your goal?
- How else could you handle these activities? Could they be delegated? Eliminated entirely from your day?
- Were there ever times when you spent time on activities that actually moved you *away* from your stated goal? What were you doing during those times?

There is, we must always remember, a big difference between being very *busy* and being very *productive.* Lots of mediocre salespeople are extremely *busy.* High achievers are extremely *productive.* Keep track of how you use your time at least once every quarter to help you build schedules that put you in the "productive" category!

Burnout Habit **#4**

Not Knowing What Kind of Day You Just Had

Learn and remember the definition of a productive selling day.

"He who only plans is a dreamer, and he who only works is a drudge, but he who plans his work and then works the plan, is called a success."

—H. Jackson Brown Jr., New York Times *bestselling author*

When you do a careful evaluation of your day, you will be able to evaluate precisely what you *did.* But you also need to find out what your activities *meant.* To learn that, you should do what I call a "meta-evaluation"—that is, determine, on the whole, whether you had a productive or an unproductive day. Salespeople who burn out, I have learned, tend *not to know* what kind of day they just had, and as a result they often give vague or misleading answers to supervisors who pose questions about the kind of day that just concluded. Just as dangerous (from the point of view of their own stress management strategies), they give *themselves* vague or misleading answers about what kind of day they need to have *tomorrow.*

When I ask a salesperson, "Did you have a good day?" I mean something very specific. When one of my salespeople tells me "no, I didn't have a good day," that salesperson means something specific, too. There's no blame or trauma associated with the simple response "no, it wasn't a good day." What matters is that we *each know exactly what the criteria for a "good day" are.* As a result, we have good information, and we know what the situation really is. We are not deluding ourselves. (See Bad Habit #1, Selling Yourself a Bill of Goods.)

What is a good day? It's a day in which at least one of the following three things happen:

- **Outcome #1:** You scheduled a new First Appointment with someone *and* you moved at least one existing prospect forward. (A "prospect" is someone who has a clear Next Step in place and is agreeing to talk with you about the possibility of working together. "Moving forward"* means progressing *either* to a state where you're talking to the right person about a clear dollar amount and a clear timeline for buying, *or* to a state where the person has given you a verbal commitment to do business.)
- **Outcome #2:** You scheduled *only* a new First Appointment with someone.
- **Outcome #3:** You moved *only* an existing prospect forward.

That's it. Those are the only three combinations for a good day. If you didn't get Outcome #1, Outcome #2, or Outcome #3 to happen today, *you had an unproductive day,* and you're going to have to try to change that tomorrow.

* **Note that "moving forward" is *not* a matter of how you "feel" about the prospect, nor is it possible, under our selling system, to consider someone as "moving forward" who has not reserved some spot in his or her calendar for you, typically within the next two weeks.**

So, let's say you were to monitor your activity over the course of a week. Understand that I'm not talking about doing an in-depth time log for that entire time; I'm talking about conducting a meta-evaluation against these three outcomes for five straight days. How many of the days in your typical selling week are productive? What did the productive days have that the unproductive days didn't? What processes do you usually follow on productive days? What simple activities (like making prospecting calls early, or adapting a simpler closing strategy*) can make it more likely for you to increase the average number of productive days in your selling week?

Every time you have a productive selling day . . . *reward yourself!* Every time you have an unproductive selling day . . . *identify something you can do differently tomorrow!*

***The simple closing technique that we teach—"It makes sense to me, what do you think?"—has the advantage of encouraging the other person to share what he or she is thinking about what you've proposed.**

Burnout Habit **#5**

Failing to Engage the Other Person Effectively During the First Meeting

Reduce those stressful first-meeting "disconnects"!

"The great mind knows the power of gentleness."

—Robert Browning, nineteenth-century British poet

One of the most stressful experiences that salespeople must deal with has to be the "glazed eyeball" syndrome during an initial meeting with a new contact. This is the familiar situation where we haven't established rapport and we're getting no meaningful feedback from the other person—and we're trying more and more desperately to "show that we know our stuff" so we get some kind of response from the person. Unfortunately, these efforts rarely pay off, and we usually conclude the meeting frustrated. We gave a great performance, and explained everything backwards and forwards and inside and out, and got no commitment for a second meeting from the other person!

The very act of trying to charm, impress, or entertain a new sales contact is likely to increase, rather than decrease, the disconnect you are getting from the person. Rather than recite the contents of your product brochure, or share long stories about your own career, use one or more of the following three strategies, and you will significantly reduce the likelihood that you will experience a stressful "disconnect" during a first meeting:

1. **Ask the other person about his or her career.** Just about everyone is an expert on, and loves to discuss, his or her own career. If you are talking to the founder of the company, ask the person how he or she decided to start the business. If you are talking to a recently appointed CEO, ask him or her how he hooked up with the company. If you are talking to a sales manager who has been with the firm for the last six years, ask how the person worked his or her way up through the ranks. If you are dealing with someone whose background or title is completely unfamiliar to you, use the all-purpose and highly effective question: "How does someone become a _____?" Your goal is to get the person to tell you a story.
2. **In the extremely unlikely event that asking the person to open up does *not* yield any meaningful interaction, ask the person how he or she made a certain decision on the job.** Obviously, if what you can ask about something that actually relates to a solution that your company can provide, you will be in a much better position to move the relationship forward. So, if your company sells industrial signage, and you've been unable to get the person to talk about career issues, you might want to ask: "What kind of signage

have you been using up to this point on your shop floor?" The basic principle here is essentially the same as the previous one; that is, keep asking until the person tells you some kind of story.

3. **If the person is still resistant, ask the person about his or her experience in dealing with companies such as yours.** In a very, very small percentage of your first meetings, you will be unable to get any reaction from the person, even though you have followed strategies one and two carefully. That's fine. Just move forward with a very *brief* description of your company and your role within it, and use this little speech as an opportunity to pose yet another question that can help you build rapport: "Just out of curiosity—have you ever worked with a company like ours before?" This will almost certainly yield some meaningful response.

In those rare cases where you're *still* unable to get the prospect to open up in any way, consider asking something like this: "You know, Ms. Jones, usually by this point in the meeting, I get a sense of what the person is trying to accomplish, and I even get quite a few questions from the other person about my company. So far, I feel like I'm not getting that kind of reaction from you. Am I doing something wrong?"

This will invariably get you a response that begins with some variation on the words, "No, you didn't do anything wrong—it's just . . ." And then you'll start to understand what's really on the other person's mind. Learning that your prospect is facing serious budget cutbacks isn't *really* stressful for you. Even if it's a short meeting, it's one where you have the chance to build a bridge and establish a business alliance. It's the meeting where the prospect says *nothing* of consequence for forty-five minutes, and then concludes the session with a terse "let me think about it" that's the real stressor. You gave your long, golden aria—and got no information and no commitment in return!

Believe me, over the course of a year, you want to have as few of those kinds of meetings as you possibly can.

Buying into the "Vanity" Sales Culture

Don't focus on yourself!

"We never listen when we are eager to speak."

—François, duc de la Rochefoucauld (1613–80), French writer

Sometimes, prospects *want* to take part in the discussion, and salespeople won't let them! One of the most exhausting patterns of selling—both for the salesperson and for the prospective customer—has to do with what I call "vanity" selling, a culture of selling in the United States today that I'm afraid has the backing of much of the mass media in support of its philosophy.

Did you ever find yourself sitting down with a salesperson who was more eager to show off product knowledge than to learn anything about your world? Was the individual focused entirely on a "performance" supposedly delivered for your benefit? Was the person so eager to get to a preplanned speech or written brochure that no meaningful questions were ever asked of you? Was the person so focused on him- or herself you could tell there was real difficulty focusing on you and what you were actually doing? If you could answer yes to these questions, you may rest assured you have encountered (or should I say endured) a salesperson who subscribes to the vanity sales culture.

We live in an era in which self-obsession is almost an article of faith. If you doubt that, consider the culture of celebrity that is so painfully obvious every time one turns on a television, or the long-winded rants of those who call in to radio talk shows, or even the insistence of major political candidates on emphasizing their own (usually tragic) personal histories or childhoods. It seems as though, in modern American culture, the only way to be a good person is to be a self-obsessed person. This phenomenon certainly extends into the world of sales.

The only problem is, vanity selling is not a particularly effective way to sell, either in the short or the long term. In the short term it tends to win you only sales you would probably have gotten anyway by walking in the door—sales with very little loyalty. In the long term, vanity selling has a way of making you hard, bitter, and more than a little cynical. People who are self-obsessed seldom come off as trustworthy, and I would be willing to bet that a fair number of them eventually become jaded and disillusioned with the profession of sales itself. If self-obsession does not lead directly to a variety of sales burnout, it definitely *does* lead to decreased performance levels that can, in and of themselves, bring on career crises that are strongly associated with sales burnout.

Self-obsessed salespeople act as though "the world revolves around me" and believe that "all customers are more or less alike—so all sales meetings should be more or less alike."

Go out of your way *not* to be this salesperson. If you fall into the vanity trap, you will only exhaust precious opportunities: opportunities to bond with another person, opportunities to find out what is new in a situation, and opportunities to identify new patterns of thought and behavior that have never been considered before.

The antidote to the vanity selling syndrome is a simple one: Ask big questions that focus clearly on what the other person is trying to accomplish, and then let the prospect set the agenda for where the responses to that question will go. In other words, instead of attempting to deliver a monologue (or just as bad, establish all thirty of the questions you intend to ask during a sales meeting, in the order in which you intend to ask them), identify three or four major areas that you really want to know about, and then *allow the prospect to direct the conversation* once you have addressed each other's issues.

If you follow this basic strategy—neither trying to micromanage your meeting nor trying to use it to deliver a long monologue—you will protect yourself against the excesses of the vanity sales culture. You will also, I believe, extend your years of satisfaction and career fulfillment as a salesperson.

Burnout Habit **#7**

Doing All the Work Without Getting Any Commitment from the Other Side

Skip the dog and pony show.

"Action is eloquence."

—*William Shakespeare in* Coriolanus

Too many salespeople we work with get hung up on the formalities of a prospect's agenda. Just this morning I had a meeting with one of our salespeople who was in touch with a major bank, and who had been asked by the bank to prepare the proposal for a meeting in January. She received this request last week. (As I write this, it is the end of November.)

Most salespeople in this situation, I'm afraid, make the same mistake that our salesperson did. They increase the likelihood of stress and burnout by assuming that they always have to play by the client's or prospect's "rules." So, in this situation, this (relatively new) salesperson would have attempted to jump through the hoop that the prospect had placed there for her by agreeing to a meeting eight weeks in the future to deliver a presentation—probably one that she would have spent a great deal of time and effort preparing.

Can you see any problem with that?

In the sales training industry, our sales cycle tends to be between six and eight weeks, from initial contact to final commitment. Here I have a salesperson who is telling me that she wants to have a meeting with a prospect whom she considers to be "active"—eight weeks from now! That is as long as our entire sales cycle takes from start to finish!

Instead of simply doing what the prospect says, it's better to find intelligent, tactful ways to win short-term commitments—and, perhaps, challenge the prospect's preconceptions. Even if the prospect is used to working with salespeople who take eight weeks to deliver a dog and pony show, or a snazzy PowerPoint, or answers to all eighty-six questions on the prospect's RFP, there's no reason why *we* have to play by those rules. We can, instead, ask to change them.

The best way to ask for a change in the "rules" is simply to tell the truth about the situation. At the sales meeting this morning, I told our salesperson that the meeting she scheduled was too far in the future, and I reminded her that people tend to agree more easily to meetings that are beyond a two-week time frame. (This principle applies to virtually all meetings in all industries.) The further away the meeting, the more likely the person will say "yes, sure, that sounds okay." However, that meeting is also very likely to be canceled at the last minute or forgotten about entirely.

I suggested that the salesperson simply call her contact, mention that she had spoken to me, and pass along my suggestion that they get together next week in order to develop ideas for the eventual meeting in January. By doing this, I was encouraging her to use a creative-stress strategy I've used countless times to escape the dog and pony show altogether. By sitting down and working out specifics of what would go into such a presentation, you can often avoid the necessities of having to give this presentation at all!

The presentation itself, if it ever happens, can be approached in much the same way. You have to sit back and ask yourself: Why am I being asked to deliver this presentation? No doubt, there are people in the room whose voices you need in order to close the sale. Why on earth would you not approach these people ahead of time and attempt to address all of their issues one on one, before walking into a conference room and making their internal debate part of your sales process?

If all else fails, and you are resolutely barred from any kind of access or interaction with the key players beforehand, and your only next step is a meeting set, say, two months from the present date, then you probably should not consider this contact to be an active lead. You are also well advised to avoid spending a great deal of time developing a proposal for this organization, since doing so would mean that you placed a great deal of time, effort, and energy into the relationship—time, energy, and effort that your prospect or client did not reciprocate. That's a great way to leave yourself open to burnout-inducing stress!

By the way, whenever I find myself in the dog-and-pony-show trap, and none of the strategies I've outlined in this chapter have helped me avoid it, I'll tell the truth about the situation once I make it into the meeting . . . and usually avoid having to make any presentation whatsoever! It works like this: I'll look at the VP—or whichever individual has invited me to speak to the group—and ask him or her, without batting an eye: "Before we get started, why did you want me to speak to the managers here today?"

Invariably, the senior decision-maker who has brought me in will say something like: "Well, I knew that the group had different opinions on the way we should proceed, and I wanted you to be able to address all their issues."

Then, without even beginning the tedious process of working my way through a sixty-eight-slide PowerPoint deck, I'll simply say, "Oh, okay. Well, why don't we go around the room and share people's concerns and figure out exactly where we stand."

This approach always elicits important information, and usually helps to build a consensus of the group. It's not as good as tracking down the individual members before the meeting and identifying his or her concerns, but it's better than jumping with both feet into a presentation that no one in the room has had the chance to critique or give feedback on.

The best reason to avoid putting huge amounts of time and effort into a presentation or proposal in advance of a meeting a month and a half or two months from now, is that doing so is extremely stressful. You invest a great deal of your own energy into something that has a very high likelihood of never even being read or evaluated fairly by the people for whom you're preparing it! Far better, in my opinion, to canvass the group either formally or informally, and develop a brief overview of golden principles that everyone can agree on. When in doubt, save yourself the aggravation. Tell the truth about exactly what you'd like to see happen next, and challenge the prospect's existing way of evaluating your proposal.

A side note: By taking this basic approach to a recent RFP that came in to our company, we were able to get a major decision-maker to completely rewrite the specifications for the program in our favor—and accelerate the sales cycle! If we had simply followed her instructions, and delivered the proposal we had been asked to deliver, we never would have gotten the business. Here's the case study:

> Recently we got a request for a training proposal from a company in the leasing industry. Instead of simply calling and saying we would forward a bid, or forwarding the bid and skipping the call altogether, I called the contact person. When I realized she was not the decision maker, I got the name of the decision maker from her, and then called the decision maker. I asked him, "What made you decide to send this to us?" I learned that we'd almost done a keynote speech for him last year, but had lost the deal. I asked some more questions. Then I said, "This request for a proposal you sent us doesn't make sense; this isn't really how I'd recommend you do the training. What made you decide to do it this way?" I learned why he had put the request together as he had, and took lots of notes. Then I explained how we typically conduct a program, and why what he was suggesting wasn't really the structure we'd recommend. He said, "Can you put together a proposal the way you'd do it?" I said, "Sure." To make a long story short, we got the deal—by restructuring the bid process to match our strengths.

—Courtesy of Steve Bookbinder, D.E.I.'s executive vice president

Burnout Habit **#8**

Forgetting about Prospects Once They Turn into Customers

Revisit your plan!

"I got a simple rule about everybody. If you don't treat me right, shame on you."

—Louis Armstrong (1901–71), jazz musician

A customer calls up his salesperson and says, "You know, I feel like we're just not that important to you anymore. When you first approached us, you told us you were going to do all kinds of great things for us. Nowadays, I feel like I don't have your attention for more than two minutes at a time. It's a big deal if I get you to return a phone call. What happened?"

"Oh, that's easy," the salesperson answers. "You stopped being a prospect and started being a customer. That's what happened. We only talk to prospects about our plans for working together."

Recently one of our trainers took flights to Chicago, Houston, Dallas, St. Louis, Louisville, Cincinnati, and New York. Now, millions of dollars' worth of print, radio, and television advertising are supposed to convince fliers that Airline A shows up on time, Airline B delivers great service, Airline C understands business travelers, and so on. But this trainer has no loyalty whatsoever to any of the airlines he took to reach those seven different destinations. The service levels he received were virtually identical. For him, all airlines are basically the same, because he can't tell you which airline's water is coldest, which food is better, which is likelier to keep its schedule. For him (and for many fliers), there's simply no follow-through on their claims. As a result, that trainer has a right to treat the airlines the way a long-ignored customer is likely to treat the negligent salesperson. He has a right to say, "You know what? You talk a good game, but you're really no different from anyone else out there. And I don't feel any loyalty toward your organization."

Before a customer moves on to the competition, we have to ask ourselves: Have we actually followed through on all the elements of the original plan? If not, we've already got a good idea of how to hold on to this customer. Good customer service really means doing what we said we would do when we first obtained the account. So, what steps can we take to make sure the customers we work with don't think of us as commodity suppliers—people to whom they owe no loyalty? Here are ten ideas:

1. **Look at your original plan . . . and think about the customer.** This is the big one. When there's a problem with your

customer, it's almost certainly because you haven't executed the plan you set up with that customer. So don't wait for a problem! Look at the plan now.

Studies indicate that we've got a one-in-two chance of getting new business from current customers, a one-in-four chance of getting new business from inactive accounts, and only a one-in-twenty chance of landing business with a brand new contact. Sure, you have to reach out to new people—but you also have to pay attention to the people who are likeliest to bring you business.

2. **Listen to your customer.** Go back to the customer and ask more "how" and "why" questions. In order to make the sale in the first place, we should have found out what the customer wanted to do. We need to keep in touch and develop more information—and figure out what we've overlooked (or forgotten) since we last discussed what was important to our customer.

3. **Suggest new ideas.** Talk to your customers about what you've come up with since reviewing the plan you both agreed to. We promised to "take care" of our customers. That means thinking about new ways we can work with them and help them do what they do better—not just keeping in contact when there's a question about billing. Suggest innovative ways to work with your customers . . . or your competition will do this for you.

4. **Keep your customer in the loop.** Let your contact know what is going on with you and your company. Keep the person up to date about all relevant management and personnel initiatives. (And, while you're at it, keep up with what's happening in your customer's life, too.)

5. **Explain what you're doing for this customer—and why.** If there's a change or improvement you've made internally to serve this customer better, talk about that change. Tell your customers exactly what you're up to, and what new processes you've implemented.

6. **Respond quickly and efficiently to both good and bad news.** Whether you're moving forward on a new opportunity or resolving a problem, take action quickly and efficiently. No matter how good or bad the situation is, do what you say you will do.

7. **Be timely and on time.** Always. No exceptions. I've run into many salespeople who assume that it's all right to cut corners with current customers as far as punctuality and timeliness is concerned. It isn't.

8. **Go one step beyond.** That means exceeding not only what the customer expects, but also what we ourselves expect. The future belongs to those who pass along more value than anticipated. Accordingly, we have to make a habit of asking ourselves: "What did we say we were going to do—and how can we overdeliver on that promise?"

9. **Thank customers for the business.** And not just during the holiday season, either. Everybody thanks customers then. Find time during the year to show your appreciation when people don't expect attention. A simple card, letter, or note will do the trick . . . as long as you make sure the whole message is devoted exclusively to saying "thank you," and not to looking for new business.

10. **Be thankful.** These people are the reason you're able to pay your bills. You need them. Remind yourself of that every single morning when you show up for work and you'll be on the right track.

Burnout Habit #9

Not Positioning Yourself as a Resource

Learn the four steps of the sales relationship.

"Avoiding failure is not the same as seeking success."

—Roger Fritz, president and founder of Leadership by Design

Imagine that you are sitting across the table from your very best customer, and you hear these words: "Here's the deal. You're out of the budget unless we get . . ."

I think you'll agree with me that these are words we really *don't* look forward to hearing from our number-one client.

Burnout-inducing stress sometimes comes about because we take customers for granted—or to be more accurate, we don't give them enough reasons not to take *us* for granted. We don't move ourselves forward toward the status of being a *resource* to our customers. We have a lot of customers, but how many of them consider us resources?

For most salespeople, interest in the relationship is very high at the outset of the relationship with the prospect, but it recedes once the sale becomes relatively certain. This is a natural tendency, because as the salesperson must always focus on developing new prospects, his or her attention is elsewhere. But notice that the pattern is exactly the opposite from that of the customer. To retain customers for the long term, salespeople must work with others to insure a constant focus on what the customer is trying to accomplish.

The sales process from two viewpoints

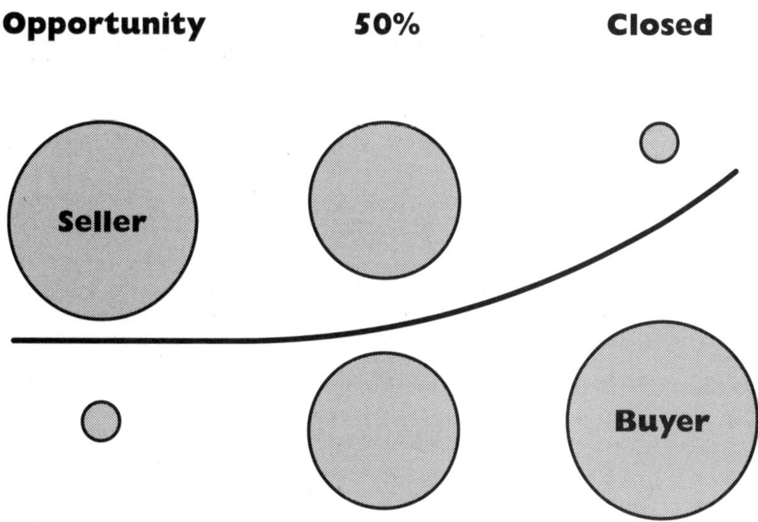

As we have seen, stressful relationships with customers often come about as a result of plans and follow-through campaigns that do not match up with the initial proposal that you as a salesperson put together. Perhaps even more important, though, is the possibility of having lost sight of the vision that you and your customer developed together as to how the relationship would unfold.

I believe that there are four basic stages to the sales relationship we have with each customer, and that they can be described as follows.

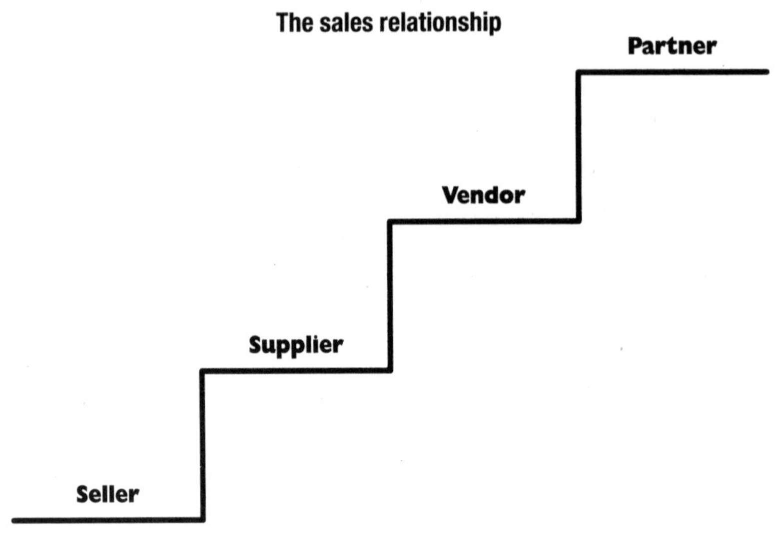

The further along we move with the customer on the sales continuum, the better our information gets, and the more valuable the relationship becomes to both parties. The four stages go like this:

1. **The seller stage.** This first and "lowest" level features virtually no trust or information; it is typically a "one-time sale" mentality on both sides of the transaction. If we don't faithfully execute the plan we have set up for the customer, or if we don't make the customer feel that we are listening just as hard after he or she signs the contract as we were beforehand, then the relationship is likely to stay at this first phase.

2. **The supplier relationship stage.** This second phase features a little trust and a little information; you are "in the Rolodex," and future business is a possibility—but not a sure thing.

3. **The vendor relationship stage.** This is a still higher phase that features significant levels of trust and information; there is predictable repeat business, and you help the customer develop criteria for doing business and resolving challenges.

4. **The resource stage.** At this phase of the relationship (sometimes also known as the *partner* phase of the relationship), there are extremely high levels of trust and information exchanged between both organizations. You really do function as a strategic partner with your contact, and you and the customer are mutually dependent on each other for success.

If you are in a "partner" or "resource" relationship, you have access to all of the key players, and you typically do not have the stress of being ordered out the door or being threatened with that outcome. If you're a resource, you don't hear coronary-inducing things like: "You're out of the budget unless we get . . ." Most salespeople go back and forth between the second and third levels. However, the best salespeople—the ones who experience the least burnout-inducing stress when it comes to retaining important clients—move most of their customers forward!

The goal of effective selling is to take the time to figure out where we really stand, learn what competitors are involved, and move toward the fourth, or partnership, level. If there's a crisis, and your customer is working with you as a resource—someone he or she has come to think of almost as a virtual employee—then the odds are good that your customer is going to call you in and strategize on how to deal with the crisis together. You won't be issued an ultimatum.

How do you know when you've reached the resource, or partner, status? Here are some of the signs of this relationship:

- You know the customer's business well enough to explain it to your sales manager and answer all his or her questions.
- You know how and where the customer's organization makes money.
- You have access to everyone you need in the organization.
- You have been working with the company for an extended period of time.
- Your contact frequently contacts you for advice, insights, or help.
- Your contact volunteers to eliminate internal obstacles for you, obstacles your competitors would probably have to deal with without help.
- You could call up the senior people in the organization and say "How's business?" and get a meaningful, extended conversation going with that one question.

Obviously, a lot of work goes into building a relationship like that, and most of the work has to do with getting *constant feedback* from your customers (see Habit #10). But this is definitely an investment worth making.

Do whatever you can to move *all* of your important customer relationships forward, toward the level of resource or partner. Don't settle for static! The more people you have in this fourth category, the less likely you will be to have customer service crises.

Burnout Habit **#10**

Not Getting Feedback from Your Customers

Stay in touch with the people who pay your commission.

> "Listening well is the primary tool of the effective salesperson."
>
> —*Anonymous*

I cannot overemphasize the importance of staying close to your customers—nor can I give you a better summary of how to elicit feedback from them than to quote the following concise list, composed by an anonymous sales professional some years ago. You could do worse than to write the list out by hand (the better to remember it) and post the handwritten list in your cubicle, where it can be seen every working day.

Staying in Touch with Your Customers (Author Unknown)

Following are twelve methods to stay in touch with your customers—and get an idea of how you are doing in *their* eyes:

1. **Ask them how you're doing.** If your business depends on customers coming to you, dedicate a percentage of your workday to mingling with them. If you travel to your customers, dedicate a percentage of your visit to collecting suggestions for improvement. Carry a pocket notebook to capture customer comments—logging them in the customer's presence.

2. **Take advantage of incoming telephone lines.** Your receptionist is perfectly positioned to capture customer comments or ask customers quick satisfaction questions. Customer service 800-number lines should have systems in place to log the problem, the solution, and customer identity information.

3. **Use customer comment cards.** Postage-paid cards are an inexpensive way to gather feedback not otherwise available. *Caution:* Make sure you follow up immediately on each card—especially complaints. Postal mail delivery time means the complaint has been simmering for days before you receive it. Customers often view no response as worse than the original slight.

4. **Use focus groups.** Gather a new group of five to eight customers every ninety days for one or two hours. Provide refreshments and remuneration, and be prepared with questions, new product offerings, and an open ear. Remember, the less defensive you are, the more you will learn.

5. **Conduct telephone surveys.** If done properly, telephone surveys can be an inexpensive way to impress customers. Most are flattered that a company singled them out for their opinions. Talk to each customer as an individual, use his or her name and any other

specific information that applies to that person. Keep the interview short—no more than five minutes.

6. **Conduct mail surveys.** A well-designed mail survey can provide in-depth information a customer would never offer to your face. Keep the questions simple, concise, and limited to one page. The more complex a form, the lower the response rate.

7. **Conduct employee surveys.** Frontline employees know your customers better than anyone in your organization. To ensure their knowledge reaches company decision makers, hold frequent meetings with employee representatives to find out what they are noticing about your customers. Rotating participants spreads recognition and adds diversity to information gleaned. Be sure to act on suggestions or employees will stop offering them.

8. **Use e-mail.** Virtually free, e-mail is extremely easy for customers to use and it arrives immediately. Check the mail often and have systems in place to immediately respond to complaints. E-mail's immediate transmission creates customer expectations of your immediate response.

9. **Use computer bulletin boards.** Post questions as often as you like. You'll be surprised at the speed and volume of comments you receive. Ask respondents to reply to your e-mail address. Most will, some will not.

10. **Put up a Web page.** The latest estimates show over 50 million people throughout the world now access the Internet. A page on the World Wide Web is not only a great selling tool but can also be designed with built-in customer response mechanisms.

11. **Send thank-you correspondence.** After-the-sale correspondence is a great time to solicit customer feedback. If a letter is mailed within thirty days, service, support, assembly, and ease of use information will still be fresh in a customer's mind.

Once again, customer feedback is one of the most important factors you need to keep up with. Consumer goals change daily and if you don't keep up with your customers' objectives, they will find a business that will!

Burnout Habit **#11**

Making Sales Projections That Have Nothing to Do with Reality

Do a reality check.

"Oh what a tangled web we weave,
when first we practice to deceive."

—*Sir Walter Scott (1771–1832) in* Marmion

You may think you're doing yourself a favor or protecting yourself by projecting your income for the next quarter "aggressively" (meaning you're setting unrealistic sales goals)—but you're not. You're only giving your supervisor unnecessary aggravation and deepening the potential for miscommunication in the relationship.

Fight the urge to oversell (or, for that matter, undersell) your income potential for the next week, month, or quarter. Be ruthlessly honest—but be honest. To get some help on making *realistic* projections, you should take a few minutes to review Beat Burnout in Your Sales Staff Tip #13 in Part Four. This is a system managers and salespeople can use to identify exactly what's on the horizon in terms of closed sales.

Burnout Habit #12

Not Making Peace with Your Organization's Tech People

Get technical team members on your side—by appealing to their expertise.

"To conquer oneself is a greater task than conquering others."

—*The Buddha*

How can we begin to catalog the many possible ways tech people and salespeople can drive each other crazy and make each other's lives difficult? Those in programming, operations, inventory, or accounting are fond of saying that salespeople make things up as they go along during their meetings with sales prospects. It is just as accurate to say that tech people have no idea what it's like to have to close sales for a living.

It is certainly true that, for salespeople, a high portion of work-related stress derives from technical problems that do not seem obvious at the time we are interacting with prospective customers. To minimize the chance of a later problem with your tech people, your accounting people, or your operations fulfillment crew, consider taking these six steps on *each and every one* of your proposals:

1. **Do not instantly answer "yes" or "no" to a technically oriented question.** It is entirely possible that the answer to your prospect's question may have changed since the last time you heard about it, or since the last time you read the company's Web page, newsletter, or technical update. If the prospect needs information that exceeds the scope of your job, tell the prospect you will check with headquarters and follow up with the details as soon as possible—then do so!

2. **Do not make stuff up.** If you have a clear sense of where the possible problems with your tech people are going to emerge, be up front about it. Do not give cagey answers or put cute little disclaimers in when answering prospect questions. For instance, if the prospect asks you whether a certain computer system will support a certain software, and you know it will not support a popular brand, the answer should not be: "We support all major brands of software, with only a few exceptions." It is better to determine that there is not a realistic match early on in the relationship than to wait for a disaster to strike during rollout.

3. **Find ways to keep in touch with your tech people.** We live in an era when technological change occurs at breakneck speed. It is entirely possible that new work-arounds, new systems, and new opportunities have presented themselves between the time you last spoke to your tech people and this morning's cup of coffee. Make an honest effort to keep up with what's going on in their world, even if you don't know a cache file from a nail file.

4. **Show any contract or proposal you are uncertain about to your supervisor and/or tech team before you show it to the prospect.** Do not tap-dance around questions you don't know the

answers to. It is all very well to paint a professionally responsible but optimistic picture when you are in a face-to-face meeting with the prospect. But if you realize after that meeting that there are huge areas where your skill or knowledge is lacking, you need to call on internal resources to straighten everything out. Try to avoid having to clean up after yourself.

5. **Bring the tech person along on one of your meetings.** This is a great reason to get together for a second meeting. (If you have read any of my other books, it will come as no surprise to you that I am big on finding reasons for second meetings with prospects.) Do not fight the fact that you have someone in the company who has a different area of expertise than you do. Use it! At the end of the first meeting say, "You know what, this sounds like a fascinating project, and I would love to find a way to get your tech people together with my tech people so we can talk about what the parameters might be. Can I come back here next Tuesday at two o'clock with our head of programming so you can meet her?"

6. **Keep tabs on the rollout.** It is possible that you may have gathered information through the sales process that will help the implementation phase succeed without any snags, crises, or nervous breakdowns.

Do not make the common mistake of assuming that once the contract is signed and the first commission check is cashed, your role in the sale is complete. If you want to turn your one-time customer into a repeat customer, you will share all the information you've gathered with your tech team, and you will monitor how the project is faring through the implementation phase.

Burnout Habit #13

Keeping Your Supervisor Out of the Loop

Keep your manager up to date.

"We have to do the best we can.
This is our sacred human responsibility."

—Albert Einstein

Your boss needs to know what you're up to—period. So don't invest a lot of your time and energy in a deal that he or she is not aware of. Keep everything above board. Explain what you have planned for the week, and get feedback and advice on how to move things forward. (See Beat Burnout Strategy #18 in Part One for advice on using your sales manager as a resource.)

In addition, bear in mind the following basic communication concepts when dealing with your supervisor (or anyone else, including prospects and customers).

1. **People respond in kind—we create the flow.** This means simply that you should choose the opening question or statement of any interaction carefully. The subject you introduce is the subject

that is the point of departure for the rest of the conversation. So if you begin a conversation by asking, "Have I caught you at a bad time?" then the initial interaction during the discussion is likely to be less than productive for both parties. The subject, after all, that you are starting with is whether or not the person has time for you. Very easy answer: no. If, on the other hand, you were to open a conversation by saying, "I had a great idea I wanted to share with you," and then shared something about a more efficient or productive way for you to complete paperwork and keep your supervisor happy, that exchange is likely to be much more productive.

2. **All responses can be anticipated.** If you worked with your boss for more than a month and a half, you can probably predict certain types of reactions ahead of time. In other words, if you have a relationship with this person, you already have some idea about what "works" and what "doesn't work" in a business setting with this person. Learn to predict the responses that you hear from this person again and again and again, and be ready to either address them intelligently or put the emphasis on a different subject that appeals to both of you.

3. **People communicate through stories.** Your goal through any discussion with your boss—or anyone else you're trying to build commonality with—is to encourage the other person to tell a story. One good way to do this is to begin by telling a short story of your own that illustrates a key point, and then to ask for reactions, parallels, or whether the person has undergone similar experiences. Once your boss starts sharing stories about his or her world, you'll be on the right track.

Burnout Habit #14

Not Instilling a Sense of Urgency

Train your prospects well!

"Remember to live life to the fullest!"

—Goethe (1749–1832), German poet

Some of the most stressed-out salespeople I know are those who haven't yet mastered the art of training their prospects. They spend the whole sales process jumping through hoops for people who don't make any parallel investment in the sales process. This is a recipe for frustration and long-term career dissatisfaction.

As professional salespeople, we have to instill a sense of urgency in our prospects; we have to "train" them to understand that if we are to work with them, it must be within the context of a specific timetable. But some salespeople say: "We can't train the people we sell to! That would be showing disrespect!" The truth is, though, that it is your actions and your choices that show the other person what you expect from a business relationship.

Think of it this way: Your garbage man has you trained. Let's say he comes by once a week, on Monday morning. He has "trained" you to take the garbage out every Sunday night, because he always picks it up on Monday. That's his action; that's what he does. He doesn't pick the garbage up on Tuesday or Wednesday; he picks it up on Monday. If the garbage isn't out on Monday morning—he doesn't care, he skips it. He has trained you to respond in such a way that allows you to have a relationship with him, and he's done it without showing any disrespect to you. Similarly, if a prospect tries to get us to invest massive amounts of time and effort on something, but makes no commitment on his or her company's part, we need to be willing to draw the line. We need to train them to behave more appropriately, by linking what they want (reports and data and analysis) to what we want (face-to-face meetings with other key people within the organization). We have to do this tactfully and professionally, but we do have to do it—one step at a time.

Make sure the actions you take "train" your prospects to understand that time is crucial in your sales process. When you start to see the sale lingering, move quickly—either win some kind of commitment for action, or move on to someone else.

Part Three

Insights

In this part of the book, you'll find specific *insights* for long-term career management—insights that help you to consolidate what you've learned in Parts One and Two and keep your career on the upswing.

Insight **#1**

Professionalism Prevents Burnout

By definition, a *professional* is someone who has mastered a skill and is truly expert enough in it for others to pay for the intelligent exercise of that skill. Here's how the *American Heritage Dictionary* defines "professional": *a skilled practitioner; an expert.* Today, the vast majority of America's salespeople consider themselves professionals. But how many really are? And what specifically does it *mean* to be a true "sales professional"?

Some salespeople make the mistake of believing that *appearing* professional is the same as *being* professional. They believe that, if they take a course or listen to a book, they'll be able to deliver some kind of inspiring or persuasive performance during meetings with their prospects. These salespeople imagine that their profession is a form of performance art. They believe that if they entertain or distract the prospect, they will get the sale. This, unfortunately, is a faulty understanding of professionalism.

Other salespeople mistakenly believe that, to be a professional in the field of sales, they must master the art of persuasion. For these people, the focus is on convincing the customer or prospect to buy. Any deficiencies the customer perceives in the actual quality of a service plan, or product, or implementation, might as well not exist to these salespeople. Their goal is to beat the competition into enticing a prospect to purchase something that he or she may or may not actually need . . . and then to move on to the next sale. This, too, is a faulty understanding of professionalism.

Still other salespeople mistakenly see professionalism as a matter of identifying problems or pain. This may sound, at first, like a good definition, but there's a problem with this approach. By asking about problems and pain, you basically *limit* yourself to winning sales only from those people who are willing to discuss their problems with you. The rest of the people are going to be "all set," and that's what you will hear, over and over again if you operate under this definition of professionalism. People who define professionalism in this way tend not to make very much money.

A better definition of a sales professional is this one: *Someone who asks questions about what a customer is trying to accomplish. What do you do? How do you do it? When and where do you do it? Why do you do it that way? Who are you doing it with? How can we help you do it better?* That's what a skilled practitioner, an expert salesperson, does—finds out what the other person is trying to accomplish as an individual and as part of a larger group, and asks questions that unearth the particulars. *This is an example of building creative stress or tension into the relationship.* The act of asking these questions tells the professional salesperson what's really going on in the other person's world.

A true sales professional is one who is willing to assume that it makes sense to move forward to the next step of the relationship with the other person, and forthrightly asks the prospect or customer to move forward to that next step—in order to see what will happen. *This, too, is an example of building creative stress or tension into the relationship.* The act of asking for this next step tells the professional salesperson about the real (not perceived) status of the relationship, and when you know what the real status of the relationship is, you're in a much better position to determine how much time or energy you should invest in it.

A true sales professional is one who verifies his or her information *before* making a formal recommendation ("Here are my assumptions . . .") and never makes a presentation on a deal that he or she doesn't believe will close. Sometimes salespeople ask me: How on earth can you tell whether a sale is going to close before you make a presentation? The answer is very simple: You ask the prospect! You say, "Listen, based on what we've gone over so far, and based on what you've told me today about what my proposal should include, I have to tell you that this is looking very good to me, and I don't see any reason why we wouldn't be able to close this when I come by on Tuesday to show you the full proposal. Am I on the right track?" *Here, again, the professional is building creative stress or tension into the relationship.*

If it's not time to close the sale, the prospect will say so, and will usually say why! Then and only then, will the professional salesperson make a responsible determination about whether his or her product can actually complement the other person's goals. If there really is a potential benefit to working together, the true sales professional will work *with* the prospect to find a way to build a business relationship that will benefit both sides.

Here's my point: *To the degree that we, as professional salespeople, build creative stress or tension into the relationship with the prospect, we protect ourselves from burnout-inducing stress!* We make it less likely that we're going to be "surprised" (or perhaps a better phrase is "brought face to face with reality") when we hear that the prospect is not ready to buy . . . or when we hear that the eight weeks of preparation we put into the proposal was all for naught, because we weren't really talking to the decision-maker . . . or when we hear that a prospect's industry is undergoing some kind of radical change with which we're not prepared to deal. These are highly stressful outcomes . . . but we can avoid them if we make the strategic decision to build creative stress into the early portions of our sales process!

Insight #2

Urgency Is Different from Anxiety

Some sales professionals find ways to make sales a satisfying long-term career, while others experience sales as a high-stress, short-term job. People who have satisfying *careers* in sales might occasionally find that they go through dry spells or have problems with particular colleagues or prospects . . . but they always seem to find ways to refocus on the fundamentals, keep their sense of humor, and bounce back. On the other hand, people who have *jobs* in sales often find ways to have an on-the-job breakdown even when times are good.

There are many possible reasons for these two different responses, but one thing I've noticed is that the people who have satisfying long-term careers in sales tend to operate from a standpoint of appropriate professional urgency; people who have short term jobs in sales tend to operate from a standpoint of perpetual anxiety.

Often, people with sales jobs (as opposed to sales careers) blame their problems on external things, like supposedly unfair commission structures, problems with a manager, or a "lousy territory." However, I believe the bigger problem is usually internal: the habit of revisiting anxiety-creating words, images, and phrases (to themselves and to others) that make perpetual anxiety more likely, and professional urgency less likely.

Take a look at the following list of phrases and see which ones best describe how you view your work in sales. The phrase in the left-hand column represents a different perspective from its partner on the right, but both deal with the same situation, framed in different ways. If you frequently find yourself identifying with phrases from the left-hand column, I believe you are operating from a standpoint of professional urgency. If you frequently find yourself identifying with words from the right-hand column, I believe you are operating from a standpoint of perpetual anxiety. Which of these two frames of reference seems more familiar?

Professional Urgency Frame	Perpetual Anxiety Frame
Agree to an aggressive schedule	Agree to an impossible deadline
Call to set a meeting	Make a cold call
Chance to defend your value	Chance to get hammered on sales
Work together to get over a bump in the road	Deal with a huge problem
Address a short-term challenge	Handle a sudden crisis
New opportunity	Last chance
Accept responsibility	Admit a mistake
Move forward/decide it makes sense to work together	Try to close a deal

In each case, the underlying reality reflected in the two columns is precisely the same . . . but the way people choose to define, describe, and envision that reality couldn't be more different. It's not too surprising that people who speak to themselves with words and pictures from the right-hand column tend to have more problems with burnout and exhaustion.

In the end, each of us—whether executive, manager, or salesperson—is operating primarily from either a professional urgency viewpoint or a perpetual anxiety viewpoint. Which viewpoint seems likelier to lead to long-term success? Which is most worth turning into a habit?

Insight #3

Everyone Has a Corporate Career Turning Point

In any business career, there are two types of career paths: the optimum career path and the typical career path. What makes the difference between the two career paths? Based on my organization's work with literally hundreds of thousands of salespeople, I believe the difference is our response to a "moment of truth" point that occurs in just about every career. This moment-of-truth event has a great deal to do with expectations. Take a look at the illustration on the next page.

You can see from this graphic there is an early phase in any career where one is "learning the ins and outs" of the position. Now, let's say the person's position is in sales. For such a person, the income level usually rises during this "learning the ropes" phase, which may last a year or so as people get better and better at prospecting, presenting, gaining product/service knowledge, and working on personal and professional development. The point of the graphic is that *expectation* is what drives achievement and financial reward. This is especially true in the field of sales. (Some people may in fact even bail out during this early phase; I have not tracked them in this graphic, because they typically go out and find other careers. What we're talking about here is people who make it past the first twelve months or so as sales professionals.)

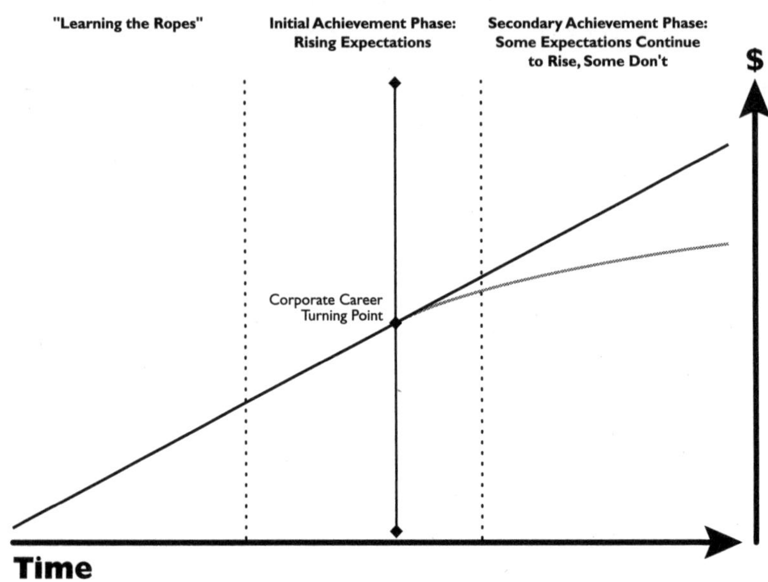

Now, notice that in the second phase the initial achievement phase expectations get higher, and income rises as well. However, I have noticed that about two-thirds through that second phase, some people's expectations start to drop off. Why? It is at this point in their careers—which typically comes, let's say, three to five years into the full-fledged development of the salesperson—that some people's incomes continue to rise, while other people's incomes level off and plateau. *This is the corporate career turning point. Some people keep setting higher and higher goals, while others settle into a routine.* How one responds to the corporate career turning point may well be the result of self-image, one's patience, or even one's ability to put the comments and questions of other people about one's career into perspective. This last point brings us to the important question of peer pressure.

Understand that, to begin with, we are all inherently social animals. No one is completely immune to the thoughts, assessments, and expectations of other people, no matter how much we would like to believe the contrary. When we tell a spouse, a parent, a close friend, or colleague that we've set a certain goal for ourselves or have the expectation of reaching a certain level of income or authority within our organization, we open ourselves to that person's opinions, which can be supportive (we hope) or not. But even so, once we make a declaration of our goals, we open ourselves up to questions about our success in achieving those goals any time that person inquires about our progress.

Suppose some person we love, respect, and admire—a spouse, a father-in-law, a close friend—knows that we have a particular goal. Let's say the goal is to earn $250,000 in a given year and to go on a long vacation to Hawaii. So when we share that goal with that person, he or she feels perfectly justified in asking us three months later, "So, are you on track for earning $250,000?" This can be a loaded question—a moment of truth when our careers are made or "plateaued"—depending on what we believe about ourselves. The question has the potential for putting us at a career turning point. Here's why.

If human beings were truly objective animals, immune from emotional or social influences, there would be no difficulty in responding to this type of question. But the cold hard fact of the matter is that receiving such questions from one or more of the members of one's inner circle can be supremely demotivating if we haven't yet made meaningful progress toward the goal, and we can become tempted to "settle" for a lesser, more easily attainable, career goal. Very often, people change their goals and downgrade their expectations and their performance after a certain point in their career . . . *simply because they believe they are more likely to win praise for attaining an easier goal that they know is within their power to achieve.*

It takes a very strong form of character to constantly shake off a loved one's skeptical questions concerning progress toward the goal. This is true, even though the timetable for the goal may not even have been exceeded, or if it has, might not have been realistic in the first place! Salespeople in particular, I have noticed, will go out of their way to avoid having to deliver frequent "status reports" to their inquisitive friends and loved ones. This is, to my way of thinking, an extremely dubious reason to adjust one's goals, but it is nevertheless quite common.

My experience is that the people who keep on some kind of upward track on the career graph are the people most committed to personal and professional development; the people who make sure they get the most support for their causes from themselves, their employees, and their families. They are also likely to ignore (or at least deflect) the implied criticisms or prying questions of friends and loved ones. They learn how to keep their own counsel about the progress they are making toward their own personal goals.

I know that this flies in the face of much advice you may have heard about goal setting. It is quite common to hear people talk about setting goals and then publicly proclaiming them so as to make backsliding difficult. I understand the logic here, but my experience in the field, having dealt with hundreds of thousands of salespeople over a period of three decades, tells me that sharing a goal with the world at large, or indeed with one's family members around the Thanksgiving table, is not necessarily the best recipe for career success.

There Are Five Stages to the Sales Career

In the last section, you saw how people sometimes plateau after completing the early "learning the ropes" phase of their sales career. Here's a more detailed breakdown of what happens as salespeople move forward through the five stages of their careers. Unlike the model in the last chapter, this model applies specifically to the sales professional.

The stages of the sales career

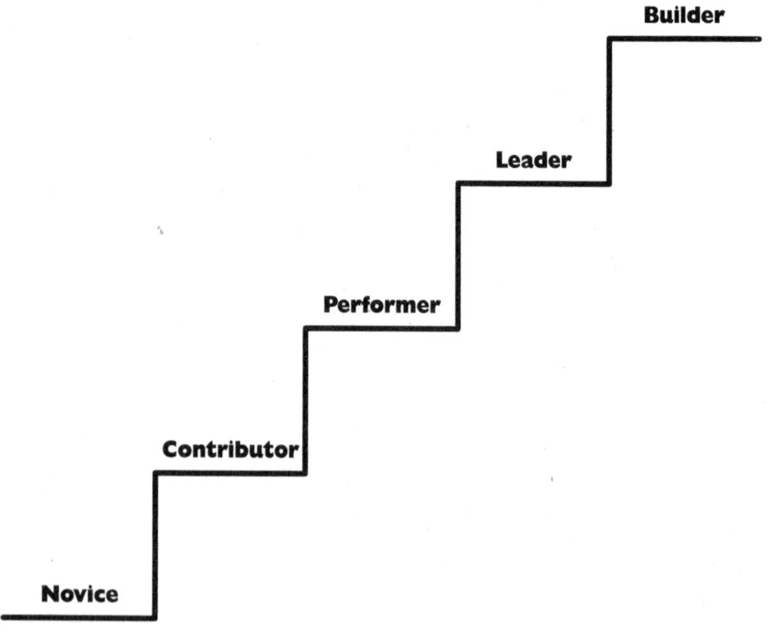

Stage One: Novice

This person relies heavily on other team members; he or she is still in the learning-the-ropes phase. The chief assets of the novice are energy and enthusiasm. His or her core requirement is the ability to learn the dimensions of the job and expand an understanding of product and service malleability. "Product and service malleability" refers to the ability to apply the product or service you sell to more than one type of use. It's usually accompanied by a greater familiarity with your organization's success stories, and a deeper understanding of how your product or service works.

A potential challenge for the novice is that he or she may place too much importance on a single prospect and neglect the importance of effective prospect management.

Stage Two: Contributor

The contributor salesperson works more autonomously. His or her chief assets are an ability to anticipate prospect expectations and the ability to manage his or her own sales cycle effectively. In addition, the contributor tends to be very strongly goal-oriented and to show a great deal of commitment to his or her work, unlike many novices. The core requirements are the contributor's ability to manage his or her own time, gather unique prospect information necessary to develop the right "proposal," and close the sale.

A potential challenge for the contributor might include not reaching out to other team members for help in securing larger and more complex deals.

Stage Three: Performer

The performer serves as a role model for others in the sales organization and assists in the completion of large and complex sales. The chief asset of the performer is a deep experience base and superior people skills. The core requirement for the performer is the ability to support and motivate other team members in support of their key goals. Performers are usually the supreme "team players."

A potential challenge for the performer is the possibility of showing impatience with less experienced colleagues. This is true of some but by no means all of the people in this category. Many performers are highly focused on helping younger colleagues learn to perform at a high level of proficiency.

Stage Four: Leader

The leader chooses to assume a coordinating role in the sales team's activities; he or she is also comfortable developing and supporting new talent. The chief asset of the leader is probably his or her ability to articulate the company vision and to support key partnerships that arise within the sales team. Many sales managers and sales executives fall into this category. The core requirement of the leader is the ability to win support for new challenging goals that are received from the higher-ups in the organization.

A potential challenge for the leader is the question of balancing work and personal spheres.

Stage Five: Builder

The builder channels his or her entire personality into the mission of building the company. Builders are so committed to the long-term success of the entire organization that they are often compared to people with religious callings or vocations. It really is a matter of faith to them that the company should overcome competitive and market challenges, grow, and prosper in the long term. Core requirements are superior executive team-building and long-term strategic abilities; high personal standards and extraordinary commitment.

A potential challenge for the builder is the perception that he or she is eccentric, paradoxical, or even autocratic.

You need not move all the way forward to the builder stage to experience a satisfying career, but you should be able to identify where you are—and where you want to be—within this model. *You should not try to perform at one level before you have mastered the proficiencies and overcome the challenges of the previous level.* I call this "stage uncertainty," which, in my view, is a source of burnout-inducing stress for many sales professionals.

Insight **#5**

It Pays to Move Forward

When salespeople do experience advances in their careers, they tend to follow the five stages outlined in the previous chapter. Some people are perfectly happy moving from novice to contributor to performer . . . and staying at that point. What's important to understand, however, is that the mere fact that someone has been on the job for a substantial period of time is *not* an indicator that the person is learning more, achieving more, or contributing more to the organization than he or she has in the past—nor is it any guarantee that he or she is experiencing career fulfillment!

Seniority does not necessarily equate with superior ability! A highly motivated young contributor may have a great deal more to offer to the organization than a complacent performer. The trick is to commit yourself to continuous improvement. In sales, careers tend to move forward—or stagnate. I believe you should always be moving forward to some newer and higher level of proficiency, regardless of what stage of the sales career you're in.

When salespeople commit to continuous growth and achievement over time, and when they consistently take actions to expand their own capabilities, I've noticed that they eventually make progress toward the later stages of the sales career, which are comparable to the levels of achievement enjoyed by the successful entrepreneur or the seasoned executive. But not everyone does that! A fair number of people plateau—and that's when job dissatisfaction and career problems can arise. If you're in this situation, it is incumbent upon you to *find a new and exciting challenge and make a personal commitment to it!* (See Burnout Habit #2: Setting Uninspiring Goals.)

Now let's look at the opposite problem. A fair number of salespeople decide to quit early in a job or career at exactly the point when they are most likely to "turn the corner" and start generating scrious income! If it takes ninety days for the typical salesperson to establish him- or herself with a company and develop enough contacts to see a meaningful rise in income, it is definitely in that person's best interests to hang tight for that time and *then* make conclusions about whether or not he or she is in the right job.

"Turning the corner": the new salesperson's big decision

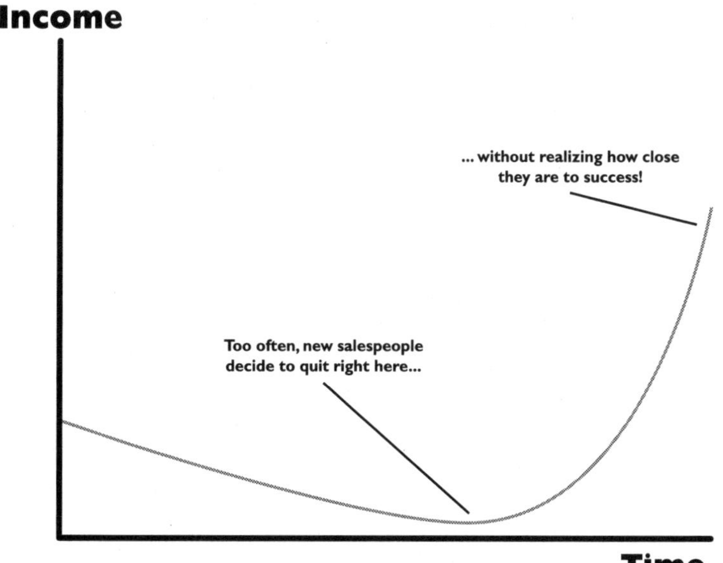

So, if you are feeling frustrated with your income performance, and you are still in the very early stages of your position with a company, you should not be too quick to bail out. I had a salesperson tell me she was ready to quit after about a month and a half on the job. I knew she had potential, and I knew she was doing all the right things. I told her, "Look, I've been down this road with people before—and the ones who succeed over time are, in this company, the ones who stick with what they're doing for at least three months. Give it an honest shot; stick around for another month and a half, and if you're still not happy about where this is going, I'll respect your decision. But for right now, I think you're going to be much better off if you give this a full-faith effort for another month and a half." She agreed. Three months after signing on to work with us, she closed her first sale.

On the other hand, I believe you should be deeply concerned if you spend *too much* time in the novice stage of the sales career. How much time is "too much" will depend, of course, on your industry and your organization's sales cycle. If you notice that a number of people with significantly less experience than you have with your company have moved out of novice and into contributor or performer, you should think long and hard about whether you're cut out for this job. Permanent novice status may, I'm afraid, be a sign that you're not likely to be happy as a salesperson, at least with this company.

Insight **#6**

Salespeople Who Don't Burn Out Have Certain Personality Traits

I have noticed that certain innate personality traits help make burnout for a given salesperson much less likely. Although you can implement particular strategies and break bad habits (see Parts One and Two) to overcome potential problems with burnout, there are certain personal traits that by and large protect salespeople from burnout. Most seasoned sales executives would agree that these traits are either present or absent—you can't train yourself to have these traits; you either have them or you don't.

I include the list of traits here because I think it may be helpful for you to review them closely and identify which are accurate descriptions of your performance as a salesperson. To do this, I recommend that you develop a short written summary of each trait you feel you possess, complete with at least two examples of times when you displayed that trait on the job. Then, put yourself to the ultimate test: Show your written summaries to a close friend or colleague, or perhaps your sales manager, and ask for his or her opinion on whether or not the trait applies to you as a salesperson!

Salespeople who don't burn out are . . .

• **Tenacious in the face of (apparent) rejection.** They have no problem pursuing a lead or a prospect who says "No." In fact, they get a large number of their sales from people who initially say "No."

• **Difficult to demotivate.** Sure, they have their ups and downs, but they're a lot like those children's toys from a couple of decades back, the Weebles. You can push them over, and they may wobble, but before too long they bob right back up to a standing position.

• **Urgent in all their communications.** These people are all about dynamism, all about moving forward. Someone who wants to stop and analyze things at length may frustrate them. A day in which no business relationship is advanced to the next stage isn't just a job challenge; it's something close to a moral lapse.

• **Curious about everything, including the ground rules.** This is a polite way of saying that they don't mind finding ways to *break* the established rules if doing so will help them to advance a relationship or identify a potential ally. (By the same token, and as a complement to this trait, they always seem to know when it makes sense to move on to another contact or another opportunity.)

• **Fanatical about follow-through.** Letters, e-mails, packages, phone calls—you name the communication tool, and they'll find a way to use it to reinforce a good impression they've just left with someone. It's not so much a matter of having a "policy" about following through; for these folks, every contact is different, and every new relationship deserves a uniquely personal touch after a face-to-face meeting.

While it's wonderful to have all of these traits, and you should certainly emphasize and nurture them if you do, only a small percentage of any given sales force will actually display all five. So don't worry if you can't claim every one of these traits in your own career. There are plenty of strategies you can master that will help you to compensate.

A side note to managers: If you interview someone who has all five of these traits . . . offer the person a job!

Insight #7

You Can't Do Everything

Sales is not your typical nine-to-five job. It's a job that you could conceivably spend *all* of your waking hours pursuing. Doing so, however, usually means inviting disaster.

You have to prioritize your opportunities, and you have to manage your own time, energy, and emotions as carefully as you manage your prospect base. Taking care of yourself is important, and a big part of that is knowing when to focus on something besides work. Here are three ideas you can use as guideposts in this area:

1. **Set nonbusiness-related goals, too.** You should have a good idea where your job is going *and* where you as a person are going. Focusing *exclusively* on your company's products, services, and customers is simply not healthy. Commit to having a social life, too, and to (gasp!) occasionally taking a day off. Set your business goals, but be sure to take a look at important nonbusiness-related priorities, as well—like those related to family, exercise, diet, and spirituality.

2. **Whittle your to-do list down to size.** Salespeople who overcommit themselves are, in my experience, prime candidates for burnout. (Often, this overcommitment problem is what keeps their commission checks smaller than they should be.) Make a commitment to learn to delegate more effectively . . . and to decline things that simply don't belong on your list. Whether or not you consider

yourself a great multitasker, the odds are pretty good that you will get more accomplished by putting your to-do list on a diet.

3. **Find a fellow "traveler" and swap ideas.** The strain of tracking down customers has a remarkable way of vanishing when you have at least one trusted peer you can talk to. If you don't have a friend or ally who faces roughly the same kinds of difficulties you do, go find one! Join a networking group, or reach out to one of your suppliers and ask to set up a lunch date with one of his or her salespeople. The act of sharing what's going on in your world—with someone who understands what you're going through—will help you deal more effectively with the latest crisis, opportunity, or sudden change in fortune you face.

Insight **#8**

You Create Your Own Truth

Each of us has grown up with certain ideas we believe to be true, certain principles we do not choose to challenge. We've adopted these beliefs and belief systems to help us fit in with other social groups, and because certain beliefs about what is "true" help us in understanding certain situations. *But whether we realized it or not, we ourselves are always the ones who determined what "truth" is relevant and accurate for us personally.* In the final analysis, no one else—no parent, no boss, no company, no social system—can determine what is true for you. You and you alone make that decision.

I've met salespeople whose personal version of the truth is that "people always try to mislead me." By focusing on that truth, they make it the central reality of their careers. I've also met salespeople whose personal version of the truth is "once I establish a good connection with someone, I usually get all the information I need." By focusing on that truth, they conduct very different conversations with their prospects than do the salespeople who assumed their contacts get up in the morning looking for ways to mislead salespeople.

It used to be true that the world was flat, that the Earth was the center of the universe, and that insects generated themselves spontaneously without parents. People believed these "fundamental truths," not because they had investigated the matters for themselves, but because someone told them it was true. As it happened, all of these beliefs—and hundreds of thousands more—were nothing more than fanciful assessments of how the world worked. They were eventually proved worse than wrong—they were proved *useless.*

Choose your fundamental truths carefully. Make sure they reflect realities you can use to summon the best from yourself and others and to evaluate the world fairly. Don't engage in self-delusion, but do work hard to build a positive belief system that supports you in every situation. *Use your own truths to discover the realities of your own world, not the world someone else told you was out there.*

Once you do this—and it may be a project that takes you years to complete—you will hold the ultimate defense against disappointment, procrastination, exhaustion, and burnout. Specifically, look with deep suspicion at any truth that encourages one of the following five behaviors:

1. Fear
2. Uncertainty
3. Doubt
4. Habits that encourage you to demand the worst of yourself, rather than the best of yourself
5. Habits that encourage you to believe the worst about other people, rather than the best about other people

Part Four

For Managers

In this part of the book, you'll find sixteen tips of interest to sales managers (or aspiring sales managers) eager to reduce burnout and turnover in their sales staffs.

Beat Burnout in Your Sales Staff Tip **#1**

Determine What Your Ideal Performer Looks Like—and Try to Hire Against That Model

It is a common maxim that 20 percent of the sales force provides 80 percent of the income for a company. As a manager, you need to figure out what, exactly, that 20 percent has in common, and to recruit accordingly. (It is highly likely that top sales performers in your company possess one or more of the five traits that help minimize burnout [Insight #6 in Part Three]; these same traits are likely to lead to long-term success and job satisfaction in the field of sales.)

Take a close look at your industry, your company, and your own top performers. Figure out what the commonalities are among the people who have been successful for a sustained period of time. If you want, you can start by profiling the people you would most like to stick around for awhile. Ask yourself precisely what these people do that other people in the organization don't do.

Make a list, and then use it to drive your interviews with people who want to join your team.

Beat Burnout in Your Sales Staff Tip **#2**

Recruit with the Live-Breathe-Enjoy Formula!

Can you remember the first time you mastered a difficult task, like learning to ride a bicycle? Can you remember something that got you so excited you wanted to tell the whole world about it? Or show off your new ability to a brand-new acquaintance? Or even give all the benefits of your new experience to someone you never even met before?

If you can remember that moment—that sense of elation, power, wonder, and confidence that came with a new discovery—then you know what kind of salesperson you should try to recruit. The very best salespeople are the ones who radiate enthusiasm for just about everything they do.

Not long ago, one of our major clients told us: "We don't hire salespeople unless we're certain they live, breathe, and enjoy their jobs. We follow what we call the LBE formula." What a great hiring philosophy! What a great way to look at selling for a living! This point of view is much closer to recruiting "true believers" for an evangelizing campaign than it is to what most companies do—which amounts to simply recruiting "average salespeople." Guess what? Average salespeople deliver average results! Is the candidate an average salesperson? Or does the person live, breathe, and enjoy the task at hand? Are you talking to someone likely to turn into a "true believer"?

When recruiting, try to target salespeople who love their jobs twenty-four hours a day, seven days a week. If they enjoy doing what they do for a living, they won't have any problem telling total strangers about it in enthusiastic terms in any social setting. This means talking to anyone and everyone they meet—the barber, the dentist, the lawyer, the person they just met at a party—about their "jobs." (And I place that word in quotes because there is usually nothing "joblike" about this kind of discussion, at least not as far as truly inspired salespeople are concerned.)

When recruiting, try to target salespeople who go out of their way to blur the division between work and play. The most effective salespeople I know don't "start work" when the rest of the world does, and they don't "quit" when the rest of the world does, either. To compensate for this apparent discontinuity with the rest of the working world, they demand a special privilege: enjoying what they do. They take a childlike joy in scheduling meetings, delivering presentations, and even making cold calls. They go out of their way to blur the barrier between work and play.

When recruiting, try to target salespeople who learn while they're in the flow (see Beat Burnout Strategy #17 in Part One). Great salespeople gather the right information—about prospects, about their own products and services, about the competition, and about nearly anything else you can name—by asking open-ended questions and following the answers wherever they lead. They don't assume that this prospect is exactly like the last prospect they spoke to. They learn by interacting, by exploring, by connecting previously unrelated pieces of information. They learn more than average salespeople do, because they keep an open mind on all subjects at all times . . . and create a flow with their questions that helps the right solutions present themselves.

Keep an eye out for the truly great sales applicant who lives, breathes, and enjoys the job. Once you find one, do your level best to win this person for your team.

Beat Burnout in Your Sales Staff Tip #3

Strategize for the Marathon

Here's a question for sales managers: How many people who start a marathon race do you guess actually complete it? The answer, as it turns out, is upwards of 95 percent! Does that figure surprise you? It certainly surprised me when I came across it.

Think of what that means. If you were to monitor a major marathon, like the yearly Boston race, and track every single one of the hundreds of participants—elite runners and newcomers to the sport, local and international entrants—what you would find is that roughly nineteen out of every twenty of those participants complete the twenty-six-mile course. That is a truly staggering statistic, given the difficulties of the task in question.

When I was first asked this question, my estimate was that approximately 50 percent of all those who signed up to run a grueling twenty-mile race would actually complete the event. I was way off. So, ninety-five out of 100 people who line up for the start of the Boston Marathon continue running until they cross the finish line twenty-six miles away. Mind you, the vast majority of them do not finish anywhere near the actual winners of the race . . . but they do finish! What on earth makes a group achievement like that possible?

Before we try to answer that question, or understand how this all relates to sales, let me ask you to consider a very different kind of race. If you were to sign up for the United States Army's elite Delta Force unit, and if you somehow made it through the initial battery of tests, exclusions, and security double-checks, you would eventually be asked to run a truly remarkable footrace. You would be gathered together with everyone in your unit and given the following instruction: "Run until you can't run anymore!"

You read right. Part of the training for entry into this elite military unit is a race that has a beginning point but seemingly no ending point. The participants are told to run until they simply cannot run any further, and they are *not* given a specific distance to run. They are, to the contrary, given no measurable goal whatsoever. They simply are supposed to run until they collapse from exhaustion. Which is exactly what they do.

Eventually, someone does step in and tells anyone who is still upright that it's time to stop running. But can you take a guess at the number of people who actually are still left running around the track by the time the officers in charge intervene? If your guess was anything like mine, it was too high. It is estimated that roughly 98 percent of the group drops out. In other words, it is almost the exact opposite of the Boston Marathon scenario. Ninety-eight out of 100 participants in that Delta Force "race" fail to complete the event. Virtually all the runners simply conclude that the limits of physical endurance have been reached. Only 2 percent keep running until the officers say to stop. Guess what else? They intervene *well before* twenty-six miles has been run by any individual runner.

So, people who run the Boston Marathon know about how far away the finish line is. And almost all of them finish. People in the

Delta Force race *don't* know how far away the finish line is. And almost all of them collapse. But before you try to tell me that the difference has to do with training and preparation, let me ask you a question. What do the two approaches to *goal setting,* specifically, tell us about the world of sales?

You get my point. These two examples suggest that managers and the goals they set for their people have a critical role to play when it comes to determining whether or not someone is going to burn out. Unless you are simply trying to identify the most hardened bodies and souls so you can take them into hand-to-hand combat, you will probably want to establish a system under which people are *more likely* to cross the finish line for you, rather than *less likely* to do so.

Unfortunately, the vast majority of sales managers in the United States today operate under what I would call an "unwitting Delta Force" mind-set. In other words, they set seemingly impossible-to-quantify (or just plain impossible) goals—not because they want to identify high achievers, but because they simply do not have the imagination or determination to identify any other kind of goal!

If you set a sales goal for someone phrased something like "you have to do better this quarter," or "you have to close more sales," then guess what? You are in an unwitting-Delta-force mind-set. You are contributing to the likelihood that the person will feel high levels of burnout-inducing stress—and eventually drop out of your team. The goal that says "you just have to do better" is like the "run until you can't run any more" goal, simply impossible to benchmark. A salesperson simply will never know when it's been achieved, because there's nothing to measure. There's no way for someone to get a sense of when he or she has reached the quarter point, when the halfway point has been attained, or when the finish line is in sight.

Now, consider the manager who says something like this: "Bill, I've looked at your numbers. I realize you're working on improving your conversations-to-appointments ratio, but based on what you're doing right now, the numbers say that we need you to make ten more dials every day if you're going to hit quota. That's fifty more dials a week. Considering your current ratios, that's two more first appointments every week. That's the number that will get you across the finish line this month. What do you think? Can you make ten more dials per day?" This kind of goal is analogous to the goal that one sets before the beginning of the Boston Marathon. ("I'm just starting out . . . I'm a quarter of the way there . . . I'm halfway home . . . I did it!")

Which, of the two kinds of goals, would *you* rather take on? Which would you be more likely to embrace wholeheartedly? Which would you consider to be more likely to encourage you to stick around with the same sales team for a while?

For someone who is currently making only five dials a day, ten more dials may be an ambitious goal (at first), but it is, nevertheless, measurable. If managers set goals like this, their salespeople will always know how close they are to attaining the goal at any given moment. If they get encouragement and support along the way, they will know when they are getting ready to cross the finish line. And they'll be much less likely to fall by the wayside.

If you want to build and sustain a sales team that sticks around, a sales team that does not burn out, a sales team that runs a challenging course for you all the way to the end, then you had better make sure you are giving your salespeople Boston Marathon–type goals that they can measure . . . rather than "run until you can't run anymore" goals that they can't.

Beat Burnout in Your Sales Staff Tip **#4**

Set Regular One-on-One Coaching Meetings

Perhaps the most obvious reason people burn out in our sales departments is their inability to achieve at a high level or to sustain their expectations that they'll get where they want to go. Some competent and motivated people, we should acknowledge, become frustrated and restless in jobs, especially sales jobs, simply because they feel they're not getting the professional support, coaching, and personal development they deserve. If they feel their career with a given company is stagnant, or that there's no realistic way to move to the next income level, or that the resources available at the company are not sufficient to guarantee their own minimum economic goals, they burn out and leave.

What's the best way around this? One good strategy is to develop a coaching plan that is tailored to the individual salesperson. Unfortunately, today's economic trends make it very likely that an individual salesperson has a great deal of competition when it comes to winning his or her manager's time, leaving any one rep feeling very much like the neglected child in a family of fifteen or sixteen. So, as wonderful as it might be to spend all kinds of quality time face to face with your salespeople coaching them through each week or even each day, that's not a very realistic possibility.

A more realistic proposition is to establish monthly or quarterly coaching sessions based on specific measurable benchmarks. In other words, try to sit down with each salesperson to determine precisely how many dials per day he or she must make in order to have a realistic chance of hitting a closing goal. The same goes for goals associated with face-to-face appointments, presentations, and closes. (It should go without saying, of course, that the benchmarks being measured in a telesales situation will be very different. They might include total conversations, total up-sell attempts, total revenue, and so on.) Then follow up on a monthly or quarterly basis to discuss the salesperson's progress and any opportunities to improve performance.

Beat Burnout in Your Sales Staff Tip #5

Choose the Mentor!

Another good strategy for minimizing sales burnout among your sales staff is to help the person find a mentor on the staff. It's better to make a conscious decision about this than to let the individual sales rep decide which mentor he or she wants to work with. To understand why this is so, consider the familiar 80/20 rule of sales. Twenty percent of your sales team is responsible for 80 percent of your sales revenue. This is a reliable rule that appears to extend across every industry. It carries with it, however, a corollary with which many managers are apparently not familiar, namely that those salespeople in the top 20 percent are frequently not in the office!

If they're field salespeople, they are very likely spending a great deal of their time on the road closing deals with new customers. Struggling salespeople, on the other hand, are likely to spend much more time in the office. This is all quite predictable, but managers often fail to realize that salespeople who are allowed to choose their own mentors will probably choose the people they interact with most, and those, by statistical likelihood, will be people in the lower 80 percent group!

So, make a conscious choice about which experienced veteran should be helping to support and answer questions from a struggling or less-experienced salesperson. Don't run the risk that you're promising new rookie will reproduce poor selling habits from a mediocre performer. Get the rookie out on the road with your top performer whenever possible!

Beat Burnout in Your Sales Staff Tip #6

Establish an Eight-Week Coaching Plan for the Team as a Whole

Effective ongoing coaching and follow-through for the sales team as a group is, I think, essential to any campaign to reduce turnover and burnout. I strongly suggest that you institute a series of weekly coaching events, developed in rotating eight-week outlines. This allows your team to receive consistent feedback on critical goals, and will also help you to inspire the team.

When coaching is an ongoing part of the sales management process, team members are more likely to "buy into" and support the coaching goals. If there is no ongoing plan, then the organization is likely to be perceived as having no direction. Remember—in hiring salespeople and encouraging them to stick with your company, you need to persuade them to follow your company's lead with enthusiasm. However, it is hard to get people to follow you if you don't know where you're going!

In the following schedule, you will find a sample outline for your eight-week coaching plan, as well as calendar sheets that you can use to develop the plan.

Week 1: Team Meeting/Overview

- Discuss short- and long-term goals.
- Identify exactly what activities will be monitored.
- Suggested activities: Ask each salesperson to write down his or her job description as he or she sees it and encourage them to discuss the results as a group.

Week 2: Monitor and Discuss

• Conduct the first coaching session with individual salespeople. As part of this, you might conduct an assessment exercise: Before the group meeting, ask the salesperson to make up a list of his or her strengths and weaknesses and submit it to you privately. Compare this list with *your* list of what you believe are the person's strengths and weaknesses. Discuss the differences and similarities during your one-on-one meetings.

• Negotiate which specific measurable areas the salesperson will work on improving over the next week.

• By this point in time, you should be collecting the information you said would be monitored in Week 1. This may be calling totals, total number of attempted up-sales, total number of presentations delivered, or any other quantifiable measure you feel is important to your selling process.

Week 3: Run a Dynamic

- A dynamic is a concept, game, or event—something that "shakes people up."

- Example: Everyone who sets two appointments today for the next week wins a prize.
- Example: Enjoy a noncontest-related group event (like a team dinner).

Week 4: Halfway Evaluation

- Discuss progress so far.
- Focus on measurable activities.
- Celebrate and acknowledge group or individual progress toward goals.

Week 5: Training

- Target the specific areas of improvement you want to encourage.
- Use training resources like books, tapes, or other internal resources.
- Encourage senior sales representatives to share their insights with less-experienced members of the team.

Week 6: Establish a New Dynamic

- Take a brand-new approach to "shaking people up."
- Use a different activity from the one you used in Week 3.
- Surprise the team! (For example: Tell them that you're awarding a special, previously unannounced prize to Joe Smith for closing the biggest deal of the quarter!)

Week 7: Progress Evaluation and New Goal Discussion

- During one-on-one meetings, re-evaluate the results of the individual strengths and weaknesses exercise from Week 2. What has changed? What has remained the same?
- Evaluate and quantify progress your team has made toward its goals.
- Work with the team to develop key elements of the next eight-week plan.

Week 8: Reassess

- Conduct a group evaluation and discussion of the final numbers that you've been measuring.
- Get feedback from team members on what worked and what did not.
- Preview the next eight-week plan and start the cycle again next week!

Beat Burnout in Your Sales Staff Tip **#7**

Understand the Transition Curve

On any sales team, there are performers whose habits we want to change. But *how* we go about trying to change those habits, and what we say and do while people are orienting themselves toward a new way of doing things, has a great deal to do with whether or not people decide to stick around.

As it happens, constructive change unfolds in certain predictable stages. Any time we are challenged to develop a new skill set, we are likely to go through a developmental process with six distinct mind-sets. In order to make constructive changes, you have to know where your people are, and how they are likely to be evaluating their situation.

Here's a model that will help you understand what a team member is probably going through while trying to change an existing selling habit.

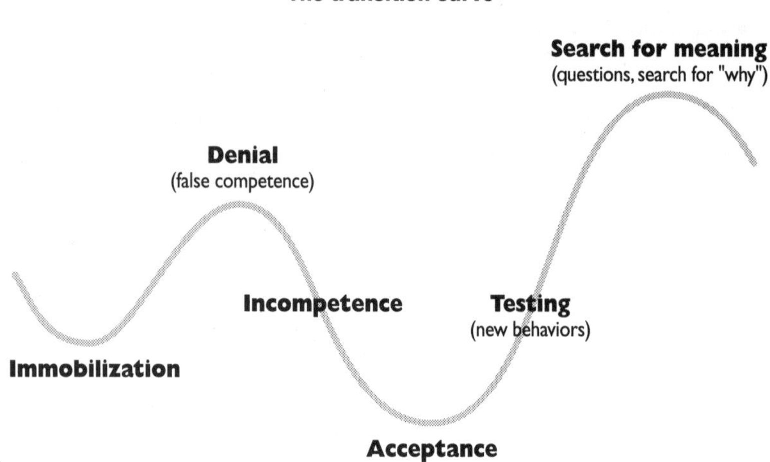

As you can see, there are five steps:

1. **Immobilization.** We simply do not know what to do, and are frozen in place. ("I don't believe in making cold calls. It doesn't work for me.")

2. **Denial.** We actively deny that any new approach is necessary. We try to improvise our way around the problem or pretend we have skills that we don't have. ("All my best business usually comes from referrals, anyway.")

3. **Incompetence.** We feel unable to improve the skill. ("I'm not going to make quota this month!") Note: If the manager does not provide adequate support and encouragement at this point in the learning process, this is a very common point when burnout-inducing stress, job dissatisfaction, and job departure occur!

4. **Acceptance.** Finally convinced that a new way is necessary, we admit that we have a lot to learn and start from scratch. At least

we are attempting to develop new abilities! ("Why don't I practice the script I read in that book on cold calling?")

5. **Testing new behaviors.** We explore the limits of the skills we are now actively developing. ("I think I'm getting the hang of it.")

6. **Search for meaning.** We start to apply the newly acquired skills to new situations and ask unique questions based on our own experience. ("What if I . . . ?")

Study the transition curve. When you work with an individual salesperson on changing a particular habit, don't expect overnight results. Help him or her to move through the stages in order, and offer as much encouragement and assistance as you possibly can during the most critical stage—stage three, incompetence.

Beat Burnout in Your Sales Staff Tip #8

Build Training and Retention Programs Around Your Top Performers

If you have followed the advice in Beat Burnout in Your Sales Staff Tips #1 and #2, then you've already identified the people on your staff whom you would most like to retain. Now your job is to implement training and retention programs that will encourage these folks (your top performers) to stay with the team.

Your goal, of course, is to *keep your top performers happy.* So make sure you pick training and reward programs that are customized to the goals and aspirations of your top performers. What will they buy into? What will keep them engaged? What will make them conclude that *you* know that they are making a valuable contribution? Remember, money is only part of the equation when it comes to determining a team member's job satisfaction; public and private recognition play a huge role, too, as do the right professional challenges.

Ongoing sales training is—or at any rate should be—an important part of any retention program, because a commitment to personal and professional development is likely to be important to your top salespeople. All too often, managers choose to focus on the potential downsides of training (like expense and logistical problems), not realizing that the benefits (retaining key performers and posting higher department sales volumes) will more than compensate if you pick the right program.

Managers have a way of overlooking the bonding effect that a good training program can have on a superior sales performer, and on the ability of training to transform a mediocre performer into a top achiever. Not long ago, our senior trainer, Steve Bookbinder, was in a discussion with a senior vice president of sales who asked him, "Steve—what happens if the top people on our staff implement your ideas, improve their skills even further, and then decide to move on to another company?"

Steve looked at him for a moment, then said: "Let me answer that question by posing another one. What happens if you *don't* train your people, and your *least* effective people don't change what they're doing, and they decide to *stay?*"

Steve got the deal. (By the way, you can learn more about training and retention options by visiting our Web site, *www.dei-sales.com.*)

Beat Burnout in Your Sales Staff Tip **#9**

Choose the Right Compensation Structure for the Salesperson

Compensation problems are, of course, a major source of job dissatisfaction for some salespeople. There has been a great deal of money spent over the last few decades in pursuit of the answer to the question: "What constitutes the best payment structure for an individual salesperson?" Nobody's come up with a single great answer—yet. However, some generalizations apply to certain groups of salespeople, and I want to share those with you in this chapter.

There are lots of sales compensation packages, but they all fall into two broad groupings that might help you determine whether or not you've got the right general package for a particular salesperson.

1. **All upside, high risk.** This package gives the salesperson an unlimited earning capacity; the company's initial investment guarantee for a particular monthly salary level is minimal.
2. **No-risk, low-income, low long-term income potential.** This package offers the lowest possible risk to the salesperson, with a cap on long-term earnings. Commissions and bonuses tend to be modest, and the level of security, at least if we think in terms of the monthly paycheck, is relatively high.

There are, of course, many variations and gray areas in between these two poles, but I'm talking in general terms about packages that tend to be offered fairly broadly across various industries. The simplest way to avoid serious money-related job dissatisfaction issues is to *align the right one of these two kinds of packages to the right salesperson.*

The low-risk, low long-term income potential package is likeliest to work best with salespeople who are just getting started in a given field. This is the approach to take for people who are not yet ready for huge fluctuations in income, and who have the potential to grow within the position.

The other payment package, the one that has high risk and higher reward, and that may entail dramatic income shifts from month to month or quarter to quarter, is best for someone with a good deal of experience under his or her belt. This is the package to offer to someone who is likely to view the absence of long-term income earning potential as a personal insult. If one of your salespeople falls into the "experienced and proven" category, and is offered a compensation package that minimizes risks and maximizes month-to-month stability, that person may feel constricted and may start looking elsewhere for opportunities. By the same token, if someone is just getting started in a given field and is eager to maintain a certain level of income stability while learning the ropes, the high-risk, high-income package is not likely to be very attractive.

If you insist on sticking with the wrong compensation package for someone, don't be surprised when that person moves on to another team!

Beat Burnout in Your Sales Staff Tip **#10**

Remove as Much Stress as Possible When It Comes to Making Prospecting Calls

Let's be honest. For most salespeople, cold calling can be extremely stressful. (At my company, we have a saying: "When God wanted to punish salespeople, He invented the cold call.") Here are some strategies for helping your salespeople master this potentially challenging component of the sales process:

- Make sound prospecting habits, including call role-playing, part of the daily or weekly routine.
- Make sure salespeople understand that they will almost certainly be interrupted when they make cold calls. Help them learn to use their script to get negative responses out on the table, then share your best strategies for turning those responses around.
- Be ready to ask: "How many dials did you make today? How many completed calls? How many appointments did you set?"
- Track your team's dials-to-completed-calls ratio over time. This number should emerge as 2:1 or lower. If your people are having problems with this ratio, find out who they are trying to reach within the target organizations. They may not be asking for the right person or title.

• Track your team's completed-calls-to-appointments ratio over time. This number should eventually emerge as 3:1 or lower. If your people are having trouble with this ratio, listen in on their calls. They may not be asking directly for the appointment by suggesting a specific date and time.

• Monitor the average length of your team's calls. If one of the people on your team is spending more than two and a half minutes on prospecting calls, the odds are good that he or she is wasting time by arguing with the prospects. Instruct the salesperson to make three attempts to turn around initial negative responses—and then move on.

For more information on the important topic of cold calling, see my book *Cold Calling Techniques (That Really Work!)*, available from Adams Media.

Beat Burnout in Your Sales Staff Tip **#11**

Understand the "Investment" You're Dealing With

Salespeople, we managers like to tell ourselves, are an investment. We tend to think of them as resources that can enrich the organization, assets that will deliver benefits to our company once we've made the initial commitment of time, salary, training, and patience. This, in my experience, is the most common outlook on sales and salespeople in the business world. It's certainly an outlook that I held for quite some time as a manager.

But the truth of the matter is, salespeople are very different types of "investments" than those we make when we write a check for a computer, a warehouse, or a delivery service. They're different because they are not predictable in the way that a physical object—or even a relationship with a trusted vendor—is predictable.

When I buy a computer, I do so under a warranty, and if something goes wrong with the computer during the time that warranty is in effect, I can simply call the manufacturer and demand repairs. If I have a problem with the delivery service, it is also comparatively easy for me, as a customer, to make the complaint or even to switch the computer supplier.

But salespeople are not replaceable parts, and they generally don't come with warrantees. They are human, and they have their good days and their bad days, and they need support. They can tell when someone takes an interest in them as human beings. They have an emotional reaction to the work that they do day in and day out. As managers, we must take those emotional reactions into account—if only because *failing* to do so will, experience teaches us, lead to high turnover rates, or even the unfortunate experience of training someone promising . . . who leaves for the competition after three or four months on the job.

In short, we managers ignore problems related to the human side of the "investment" in our salesperson at our own peril.

It is definitely in our interests, and in the interests of our companies, to support and coach our salespeople in such a way that burnout is the exception, rather than the rule. The best way to do this, I think, is simply to learn about and take an active interest in the person's life outside of the workplace. Do we know what each of our salespeople is receiving in terms of family support? Do we even know what kind of family the person comes from? Do we know where he or she lives? What his or her hobbies are? Whether the salesperson is married or has children, and if so, what the actual names of these close family members are? Do we remember these things, or do we have to be prompted?

It may seem like a transparently simple step to take a *genuine* interest in such matters, but it is, all the same, a step that many sales managers omit. Don't be one of them!

Beat Burnout in Your Sales Staff Tip #12

Learn the Criteria of the Prospect Management System

How do you, as a manager, make accurate, meaningful sales forecasts that keep your staff's stress levels to a minimum? The answer to this perennial sales question is to be found in something I call the Prospect Management System.

In Beat Sales Burnout in Your Sales Staff Tip #11, I made the point that salespeople are not an "investment" in the traditional sense. In other words, they are not quantifiable resources that can be relied upon to deliver a certain value at a predictable rate over time, and they don't come with warrantees. They are human beings, and they are hard to predict. If we *could* determine exactly what they would do over the coming twelve months, in the same way we could determine what a computer system would be capable of doing or what the capacity of a warehouse would be over a given twelve month period, life would be a great deal easier for us!

As it stands, though, we are faced with the challenge of managing a group of unpredictable human beings whose job it is to either develop new customer relationships or make the most of existing ones. Sales, we should acknowledge, is a difficult and unpredictable line of work with many emotional ups and downs. It is a fertile breeding ground for frustration and the willingness to settle for mediocrity. (See Insight #3 in Part Three, on the corporate career turning point.) Consider the common situation of a salesperson who realizes that he or she is not going to make quota this quarter, and who "saves" a promising prospect for the next quarter when he or she stands a better chance of meeting the sales goal. This "strategy" fails to take into account the fateful question of whether the prospect in question will seek out our competitors in the interim!

In response to such problems, I developed a system for managing prospects known as the Prospect Management System. It is the centerpiece of the "Getting to 'Closed'" program, which we have trained to thousands of organizations around the world. Basically, this is a simple system that helps to deliver greater forecasting accuracy, early identification of performance problems, reduced wasted time, and greater revenue for sales teams in virtually all industries. The system, which has been adopted by some of America's most prestigious companies, is, I believe, as close as any sales manager can get to turning the members of his or her team into "quantifiable" entities. It is not perfect, and it does require a system of continuous group review. But it is a proven method for changing the sales culture at just about any kind of company, and for delivering accurate sales forecasts.

So, what is the Prospect Management System? Basically, it breaks down into a six-category display that gives those who use it a visual inventory of everything that is currently being worked on by a sales team. The "team" can be as small as a single salesperson reporting to a sales manager, or as large as many regional offices all reporting to an executive at a centralized headquarters location. Here is what the system looks like:

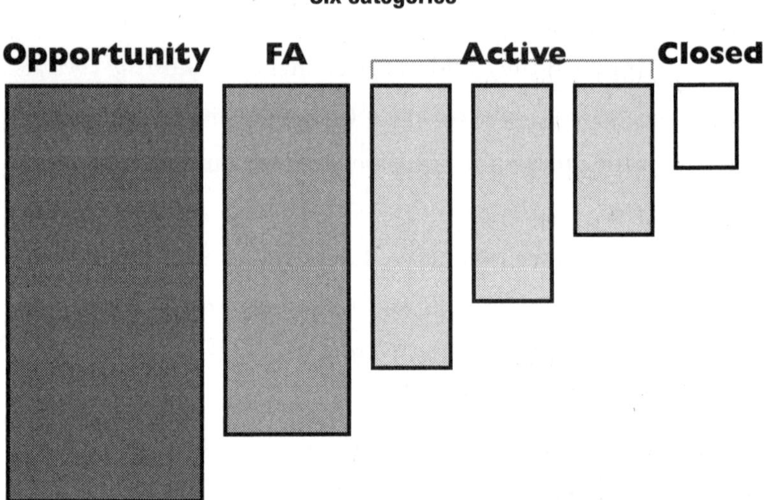

You will notice that at the left-hand side of the display in the "Opportunity" column—which we tend to display on a portfolio or magnetic board—are leads with no clear Next Step, leads that we refer to as inactive. So, the simple fact that I know that there is a company in my territory that I could conceivably work with, does not automatically make that contact an active lead. In order for that company to be considered an active lead in the system, I must have some kind of Next Step scheduled with the person within two weeks. If any contact fails to live up to this standard, it must be removed from the active section of the board—those three columns to the right—and placed in the opportunity column. Notice that the opportunity column is quite large.

Immediately to the right of the opportunity column is a column labeled "FA." This stands for First Appointment. Contrary to what you might think, this column is not yet an active lead—not technically a "prospect." These are people with whom I have spoken, typically on the telephone, and set a first appointment. But we do not consider them to be active prospects, because we have not yet met with them, and we really have no relationship yet. (As any salesperson with even a week's experience can attest, the simple fact that one has scheduled a meeting with a contact is no proof that the person is an active lead . . . . or indeed will even show up at the time and place specified when you set the appointment!)

The next columns are the three active ones in the middle: 25, 50, and 90. These have clear criteria that equate with a 25 percent, 50 percent, and 90 percent chance of closing the sale. Let's look at the 50 percent column first, because it is a little easier to explain the other two once you understand the criteria for that column.

In the 50-percent column, we classify a prospect as having a half-and-half chance of working with us. We say this, not because of a "hunch," but because the prospect meets certain predetermined criteria. We should place someone in the 50-percent category if we are . . .

- Talking to the right person.
- Talking about the right plan.
- Talking about actual dollars within a budget that makes sense to the prospect.
- Working within our average sales cycle. (In other words, if it takes us six weeks to close the sale, we should still be well within

that time window when we consider a prospect to be at the 50-percent stage.)

For this person to be considered an active prospect, we must consider the question of the Next Step. If someone fulfills all the 50-percent criteria, but has agreed to no further meeting or discussion with us, that person is technically *not* a prospect, and must move back to the opportunity column on the board, the far left-hand column. Once you understand the criteria for the 50-percent column, it is relatively easy to get a sense of what is happening in the 25-percent and 90-percent columns.

The 90-percent column features prospects for whom all of the 50-percent criteria apply—*and* there is a clear and explicit verbal commitment to do business with us. We describe this column as "C.O.D."—contract on desk. We are simply waiting for the paperwork to come back.

By contrast, the 25-percent column applies to those prospects with whom we have a Next Step, and with whom we have met at least once, but from whom we are still gathering information. So the 25-percent column is one in which we have some kind of forward movement and a commitment to future action, but we are *missing* one or more of the criteria in the 50-percent column.

At the far right-hand column of the system is the "Closed" column. This is what we're working toward. The criteria for closed sales will vary depending on the industry, and each company has its own criteria for what constitutes a close. In our company, when we receive a contract, we typically consider the sale to be closed.

Beat Burnout in Your Sales Staff Tip **#13**

Use the Project Management System to Develop Forecasts Based on Reality, Not Guesswork

So much for the categories of the Project Management System. Now, why are we and the members of our sales team bothering to commit all of these criteria to memory? To answer that question, let me pose some additional questions. Can you imagine running a weekly sales meeting where . . .

- There is a significantly larger number of first appointments and prospects in place than there are right now?
- The team focuses on strategy and how to move relationships forward, rather than on whose fault it is that a given deal did not come through?
- Forecasts actually bear some relationship to the actual sales results salespeople propose?
- Prospects move forward more quickly through the sales process than they do in your current process?
- You have a visual inventory of all current activity of all your salespeople?

Under the Prospect Management System, that is precisely the kind of sales meeting you can have. Once you and your team adopt the same vocabulary for classifying leads, you will find it much easier to work together productively as a team. And you'll generate much more accurate forecasts.

Typically, the way the average salesperson works his or her sales process looks something like this:

Slapshot selling

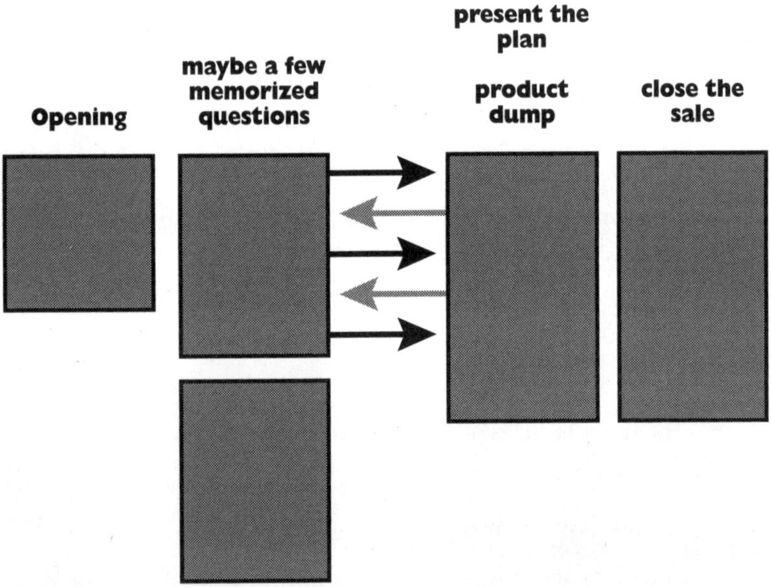

(Note, please, that we are looking at an *individual* sale, and not at a display of the entire activity of someone's Prospect Management Board.)

On the left-hand side, we have a brief opening where the person supposedly "gains rapport," perhaps by complimenting the contact on the office, or making some remark about the weather. After this initial meet-and-greet phase, the salesperson rushes ahead and poses a few superficial questions, usually the exact same ones over and over again, regardless that this contact is totally different from the last contact he or she met with.

At that point, this salesperson delivers a "product dump"—a lengthy monologue about the features of the product or service he or she sells. We also call this act of delivering a product or service-based monologue "throwing up on the prospect." It's a perfect example of "vanity" selling. (See Burnout Habit #6 in Part Two.)

At some point shortly following this performance, the salesperson presents a plan—again, usually one that's identical to the plan presented to the person he or she met with yesterday. Then the salesperson attempts to close the sale by using a variety of psychological "tricks" or "closing maneuvers" meant to get the person to overlook the fact that no meaningful information about his or her situation has been gathered. Not surprisingly, this often does not work on the first try, and so people typically spend a great deal of time presenting the plan, attempting to close it, then having to go back and present again based on little or no information.

There's a whole lot wrong with this way of selling, but I want to focus briefly on just *one* aspect of this philosophy that makes life very difficult for sales managers. The challenge is that the projections for the individual salesperson (and, for that matter, the team as a whole) are typically based on bad (or no) information! These "projections" are typically based on the salesperson's own personal feeling of whether or not a meeting "went well" or not. This is a totally subjective assessment, of course, and as we all know, salespeople routinely inflate the likelihood that a given deal will close. They often seem to follow the logic that *anyone* with whom they have met once has a 50-percent chance of buying from them, when this is clearly, as a matter of statistical fact, untrue. Salespeople meet with many, many people over the course of the year, and only a small percentage of that total ever buy from them.

A tip-off that problems in projecting income are habitual comes when we, as managers, hear the same things over and over from salespeople. For instance, the salesperson might say "I am just about to close that deal!"—but nothing actually moves forward in the relationship for the next three weeks. Or, to use another common example, the salesperson informs you that the sale has in fact closed—but nothing ever materializes, and the relationship somehow does not turn into revenue. These are both signs of salespeople attempting to sell—and project—by means of very little information on the selling process.

The Prospect Management System makes selling in this way difficult, if not impossible. Look again at the graphic.

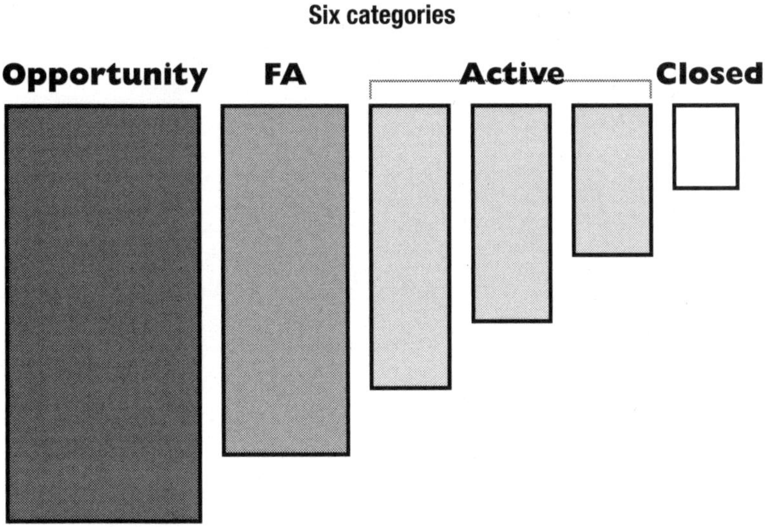

Six categories

Opportunity FA Active Closed

To take part in the weekly sales meeting, the individual salesperson has to set quotas not only for the total number of sales he or she wants to close, but also for the total number of *appointments* necessary to deliver those sales! You can also establish intermediate quotas for everything in the active categories, 25 percent, 50 percent, and 90 percent.

This one simple fact—that the Prospect Management System holds salespeople accountable not only for closes, but for all the intermediate steps that go before the close—has revolutionary implications for the way a sales team operates. It means that salespeople have to be more honest with themselves and their managers, and in doing so, have to provide information *much earlier.* This reduces stress and makes the information the team gets much more reliable.

So, to generate an *accurate* sales forecast for the next six weeks (assuming your organization has a six-week selling cycle), all you would have to do is . . .

1. Total up everything in the 25 percent column and multiply by .25.
2. Total up everything in the 50 percent column and multiply by .5.
3. Total up everything in the 90 percent column and multiply by .9.
4. Add items 1, 2, and 3 together.

That's it!

Let me emphasize a particularly important point. By the time a salesperson is able to get a lead into the 50 percent column—for which there is, if you are using this system correctly, a clear numerical quota each week—that salesperson has to tell the manager a dollar figure that he or she believes the deal is worth, a reason for why this deal is worth that much, and a likely time line for implementation or roll out. As a result, managers know exactly who is (and who is not) talking to real decision-makers! If that's not a remedy for *sales manager* burnout, I don't know what is.

Beat Burnout in Your Sales Staff Tip #14

Make "Faking It" a Thing of the Past

You cannot fake your way through the Prospect Management System. If a salesperson simply does not know the answers to the questions that will allow him or her to place a lead in the 50-percent column, the salesperson will have no leads in that column, and will have a tough sales meeting. But even the difficulty of that sales meeting is far less stressful than waiting eight weeks and being asked why he or she is so far behind quota!

What's more, any lead that is dormant for too long "falls off the board"! Remember, to remain in the active column, a lead must be playing out according to your average selling cycle. If it fails to do so, and the salesperson still has a lead up for the ninth or tenth week, when the selling cycle is six weeks, the manager is perfectly within his or her right to drop the lead back to the inactive column, thus increasing the number of new leads that this salesperson must somehow deliver. In the final analysis, the Prospect Management Board is the ultimate incentive to prospect effectively. It is a reality check that delivers an accurate message about who is prospecting and who is not to everyone on the team—and it does this well before an income crisis presents itself.

The bottom line with the Prospect Management System is it significantly reduces stress for your sales team—and for you!—by making your people focus closely on the prospecting and presentation portions of the sales cycle, and not simply the closing stage. By setting clear quotas for first appointments, 25-percent leads, 50-percent leads, and 90-percent leads, the system makes the quota for closed sales attainable. It also provides a clear demonstration of what the individual's—and the team's—actual closing ratios are.

Through this system, managers find out about problems *before* they forecast revenue, *before* the salesperson falls behind quota, and *before* the sales rep wastes time presenting a solution to an obviously unqualified lead. By holding the person to *all* the quotas, you severely reduce the likelihood the person will spend a significant portion of his or her time talking to people who have no real decision-making authority. Verified information delivers a much more efficient sales process in the Prospect Management System.

Telling the truth about where the salesperson really is at any given moment in terms of his or her prospect base is an important dose of reality. This kind of reality can transform a sales career—by focusing the salesperson's attention on what is actually taking place, not on what he or she believes, wishes, hopes, or imagines is taking place. Most salespeople react very positively to this approach and feel deep gratitude for managers who implement and support the system over time. After all, it gives them clear, measurable benchmarks that they can work toward, and identifies the *specific behaviors* that lead to success.

Salespeople who make a habit of using the Prospect Management System are more satisfied, less likely to feel out of control of their income pictures or their careers, and more likely to enjoy better relationships with their colleagues than salespeople who don't. It is, I believe, the ultimate stress reduction tool for both salespeople and sales managers.

To learn more about how to implement the Prospect Management System in your organization, visit our Web site: *www.dei-sales.com.*

Beat Burnout in Your Sales Staff Tip #15

Conduct a Call Blitz

There are a lot of different possible reasons for high stress and burnout on the job for salespeople, but among the most easily preventable is the "ups and downs of selling" cycle we have discussed at various points in this book. There is a very simple way to get around this problem and I will outline it briefly in this chapter.

When we conduct our day-long training programs, we typically set aside a specific period of time that's devoted exclusively to the activity of calling prospects and trying to set first appointments. This is a *group* activity that is highly motivating and gets everybody motivated and on the same page. Suddenly, people are enthusiastic about a task that is frequently postponed or attempted only haphazardly.

So, if you are truly interested in overcoming the potential problem of having major income swings in your sales team, the two steps to follow are these:

1. Acknowledge that steady regular prospecting is the best antidote to avoiding income fluctuations.
2. Conduct a call blitz.

Schedule a one-hour period where absolutely nothing else takes place in the department except for picking up the telephone, calling from a predetermined lead list (that part is very important, for reasons we will examine in a moment), and scheduling first appointments for at least sixty minutes straight.

In the calling blitz, it is extremely important to make sure that nothing else other than making telephone calls is taking place. So, for instance, if your team is tempted to "research" a company between their phone calls, don't allow them to do it. (This will give you an idea of the integrity of your lead list!) Have the team prepare the list the night before or the morning before, then instruct them to hit the phones and just dial numbers until everyone hits the one-hour mark.

Make this a *group* activity. Monitor dials, completed calls (conversations with decision-makers), and total first appointments. Review the numbers after the call blitz. Give plenty of high fives at the end of the session to the people who schedule new first appointments, and get feedback from the team as a whole about what worked and what didn't.

I believe you will find that these group calling efforts are major determinants of job satisfaction, and that they help avoid stressful income fluctuations experienced by your team.

Beat Burnout in Your Sales Staff Tip #16

Ask Questions to Get to the Underlying Reality of the Sale

Planning a week, month, or quarter around bad or incomplete information is stressful for salespeople. Planning the same week, month, or quarter around accurate information is much more satisfying, and much less likely to lead to burnout. So, make a point of illuminating the reality of anything and everything a salesperson is working on! The only reliable way to do this, I have found, is to ask your salespeople good questions like . . .

- When did you first meet with this prospect?
- Are you going back?
- What is your Next Step? (Get a date and time!)
- What will you take back with you?
- What's your strategy?
- Why have you let so much time go by (if appropriate)?
- What is the potential dollar value?
- What are some ways we can work together as a team to move this along?
- Who is the decision-maker?
- Who is the president/owner?

- Did you call the prospect or did he or she call you?
- How many people are involved?
- What's the contact's position at the company?
- How did the contact get the job?
- Did he or she want the job?
- About how old would you say he or she is?
- How long has he or she been with the company?
- Does he or she make the final decisions? How do you know?
- Who else is the contact talking to?
- How did the contact choose the previous vendor or supplier?
- How many times have you been there?
- What do you think will happen?
- (If salesperson says it will close) Would you bet your paycheck on this?

These kinds of questions are what I call "reality check" questions. They are opportunities for you, as the manager, to introduce some *creative* stress into the sales process internally, during every weekly sales meeting. Use them!

Appendix

Thoughts on Burnout Prevention for Telesales Professionals

The advice in the main part of this book is directed toward sales professionals as a group, but there is one subgroup particularly prone to burnout-inducing stress, and that is the group of salespeople who sell goods and services over the phone.

There are many different kinds of telesales professionals, but most of them have one thing in common, at least in the United States: They are going through a difficult passage. They face increasing regulation and even public hostility toward their profession. I believe that telesales is an honorable way to make a living, and that people who choose this line of work deserve to be treated with dignity and respect. I also believe that they deserve advice on how to succeed over the long term in their chosen line of work, and to that end offer the following suggestions exclusively for them.

A Different Way of Selling

Whenever we do programs with telesales professionals, the first thing we do is let them know that we understand their job is among the hardest jobs in all of sales. It doesn't take too much effort to see why this is so. Consider, for instance, the following facts:

- The average telesales professional gets more "no" answers in a single hour than a field salesperson gets in a week.
- The severity and intensity of the "no" answers is generally greater than those encountered by face-to-face salespeople.
- Telesales professionals do not get the same recognition as their field sales counterpart.
- Telesales professionals do not get the same career opportunities as their field sales counterparts.
- Telesales professionals do not make the same amount of money as their field sales counterparts.

And let's not forget that the face-to-face salesperson generally has an easier time negotiating an initial meeting, even if he or she has never met the prospect before. The telesalesperson, on the other hand, must be ready for a huge variety of unexpected and often disorienting responses. Some of them are positive. Most of them, however, are negative. It can be extremely difficult to get your bearings in this line of work.

It is much, much easier for telesales professionals to fall into a rut, because salespeople in this group go long stretches of time when they hear virtually nothing but intense, negative, and even abusive "no" answers. Because of this, it can be very difficult for telesales professionals to step back and distance themselves from their daily routine, and they may begin making calls under the expectation—

not entirely illogical—that the next person is probably going to offer an intense rejection, too. As understandable as this reaction is, it is extremely dangerous for any salesperson to think that way, because letting the results of the last call leach into this call is a great way to encourage the other person to deliver the rejection you want to avoid. Mind-set is all important!

Actually, this is not a complete summary of the many reasons why telesales is easily the most difficult job in all of sales. A full list would take up too much of this book, and would have to include a discussion on how major news stories and political campaigns these days are built around fomenting dislike of telesales professionals! Therefore, I address here what I feel are the most important issues uniquely relevant to the telesales world. At the same time, I suggest that anyone interested in making the most of his or her telesales opportunities get in touch with my organization, D.E.I. Management Group (*www.dei-sales.com*), and arrange for a free subscription to our newsletter, *The Executive Sales Briefing,* a quarterly newsletter that features many articles of interest to telemarketers.

Your first and most important step, however, is to accept that telesales is a fundamentally different way of making a living than other kinds of selling, and to acknowledge that the "rules of the road" as they apply to telemarketing professionals are a little different. *How you think about yourself and your job is vitally important.*

If you follow the simple steps you're about to read, you will be in a much better position to pace yourself, make the most of your phone interactions, and match what you offer to what's really happening in the lives of your prospective customers. And you'll be happier and less stressed-out on the job.

Step 1: Schedule Your Telesales Day Differently

The question of how to approach the day for telesales professionals is particularly important. Field salespeople can break up their day or week with off-site visits to prospects' offices and trips to tour their facilities. Most telesales professionals can't, and that can become a significant problem. Because they operate in this different environment, telesales professionals have to keep some specific points in mind as they schedule their day:

- **Don't try to run a marathon.** In other words, you should certainly block out portions of your day and fill them with bursts of calling activity. But you should also break up your day with periods of less intense, less emotionally challenging work. You might, for instance, choose to spend half an hour making a certain type of call and clustering together as many as you can. You might then schedule half an hour to review e-mails, update your contact base, and so forth, before returning to your calling activity. Warning: If you're tempted to multitask, don't—it never works! Do not try to make calls at the same time you're managing your paperwork or doing other tasks. When you're making calls, focus on the calls and the calls alone. Because the potential for stress and burnout is so very high, you should either be "on" or "off"—at least when it comes to making calls. You should not attempt to be "kind of on" all the time.

• **Do not call for too long.** Try to make your calls between forty-five and fifty minutes for every hour and take a break to do some other activities during the rest of the hour.

• **Keep calling right after you've had a bad call.** This may seem counterintuitive, but by postponing the next call after somebody beats you up you increase the likelihood that you will postpone placing the next call, or dread it when you do place it. You are a professional. Like a doctor or a lawyer or a professional football player, you sometimes face situations that are challenging or disorienting, or both. But that doesn't mean you should withdraw into a little cocoon while you're still in your on-the-job "prime time" mode!

Step 2: Personalize Your Telesales Interactions

Try, at all costs, to "humanize" the call. By this, I mean to say that you should find a way to draw parallels between what is going on in your world and what is going on in the prospect's world, even if doing so is not entirely sales specific. So, for instance, if you're selling magazine subscriptions, at some point during the call, you might want to mention that your own children enjoy reading a magazine you represent that is designed for young people. This kind of person-to-person approach can go a very long way toward reducing the incidence of burnout-inducing stress you experience during the course of the average day.

Step 3: Schedule a Daily Workout

Of course, this is a good idea for everybody, but it is a particularly relevant and important step for telesales professionals.

Telesales can be a very sedentary job if you let it, and the fight-or-flight syndrome can be particularly dangerous to your outlook if your job description requires you to sit in one spot for a great deal of time and talk to people who may be hostile. Break the pattern. Get outside for a walk or a jog during lunchtime or some other period of the day.

Step 4: Oil the Equipment!

Your voice is everything! Keep a glass of water nearby to keep your composure and to keep your throat and mouth moist.

Step 5: Always Ask the Other Person What's Changed in His or Her World

This is particularly important on incoming calls. If someone contacts you to place an advertisement designed to sell a motorcycle, you should ask the person what made him or her decide to call you in the first place. After all, the person didn't call because there was nothing better to do. Did the person recently decide to move to another city? If so, are there other items he or she is interested in selling? By asking about the motivation for the call, or about what took place recently in the other person's world, you will gain more meaningful information. By citing parallels between the other person's recent experiences and your own, you can also do a better job of "humanizing" the call (see step 2).

Online Resources: Stress and Burnout

These Web site addresses are accurate as of July 2004, via Google.

About.com—Stress

http://stress.about.com

Stress, stress-induced conditions, and managing stress, including research on medical conditions related to stress and tips for its control and management. Also self-assessment tools, articles, links to hundreds of choice sites.

Activekarma.com

www.activekarma.com

Information, articles, and tips on stress management.

Alternative Stress and Relaxation Solutions

http://stress-management.net

Stress, relaxation, and stress relief solutions and information including personal counseling and corporate programs. Links to other stress-relief therapies, products, and programs.

The American Institute of Stress

www.stress.org

Details ways to identify and manage stress effectively.

Anyone Listening?

http://hiswinners.info

The stress-relieving, entertaining truth behind those wise and witty one-liners you often hear.

Are You Burning Out?

www.docpotter.com/bo_quiz/bo-ami.html

Self-assessment quiz to determine the degree to which you are vulnerable to burnout.

AskMen.com—Dealing with Stress

www.askmen.com/sports/health/26_mens_health.html

Includes information and tips on dealing with stress.

Burnout Inventory: Are You Headed Toward a Burnout?

www.psychtests.com/burnout.html

A free online-scored burnout test.

Burnout Prevention and Recovery

http://web.mit.edu/afs/athena.mit.edu/user/w/c/wchuang/News/college/MIT-views.html

A short but interesting checklist of steps to consider for conquering burnout.

Clarity Seminars—Corporate Stress-management and Meditation Training

www.clarityseminars.com

Stress-management and meditation training for corporations and government agencies.

Crazy Colour Office Survival

www.crazycolour.com/os/

Handbooks, advice, forums, tools to help you at work.

The End of Stress As We Know It, 2002

www.nap.edu/catalog/10247.html

The complete text of Brian McEwen's book. Covers responses to stress; its relationship with the cardiovascular system and brain; and ways of dealing with it.

eStress.com

www.estress.com

Solutions and articles on stress, carpal tunnel, headaches, sinus trouble, and back pain.

FitnessZone—Stress

www.fitnesszone.co.za/stress.htm

Featuring articles on stress, healthy living, and wellness. Includes links, products, services, and other stress-related information.

Get a Grip on Your Life

www.get-a-grip-on-your-life.com

Learn how progressive relaxation, meditation, and self-hypnosis can help you cope with the stress of everyday life.

How Close Are You to Burnout?

www.aafp.org/fpm/970400fm/lead.html

Learn how to control stress before stress controls you. An article from *Family Practice Management*, by Janine Latus Musick.

How Families Can Deal with Stressful Times

http://healthlink.mcw.edu

Article regarding cocooning as a family-based, stress-coping strategy.

How to Survive Unbearable Stress

www.teachhealth.com

A free, illustrated Web book explaining stress, depression, anxiety, and drug use, by Steve and Kimberley Burns.

Journeywoman

www.journeywoman.com/journeydoctor/stressmanagement.html

Stress management on the road. Lee Ronald, founder of the Women's Travel Advisory Bureau (UK), shares her thoughts on the topic of women, solo travel, and stress management.

Ladies Home Journal: Relaxation Techniques

www.lhj.com/home/Relaxation-Techniques.html

Relaxation and stress reduction tips and techniques.

Lifeclinic

www.lifeclinic.com

Articles on stress reduction exercises and stress management.

Links to Stress-Related Resources

www.imt.net/~randolfi/StressLinks

Links and resources regarding stress (its psychodynamic, biological, and behavioral roots), stressors, emotional and mental health, relaxation, meditation, hypnosis, cognitive restructuring, biofeedback, REST (restricted environmental stimulation technique) flotation, and stress research.

Mastering Stress

www.masteringstress.com

Self-help stress reduction program that assists people in developing effective strategies to combat stress.

MerckSource—Managing Stress

www.mercksource.com

Illustrated guide providing information on causes, effects, and tips for managing stress.

NOSTRESS4u.com: Psychologist Henrik Brandt

www.nostress4u.com

Stress, stressors, stress coping strategies, stress detection and etiology.

On Top of Stress

www.speaking.com/articles_html/SherylGrimme_892.html

Brief article by stress management trainer Sheryl Grimme describing how individuals and organizations can "beat stress before it beats you." Includes six steps to assertive behavior.

Pioneer Thinking—Trauma and Worry

www.pioneerthinking.com/trauma.html

Trauma, worry, and stress—physiological and psychological effects.

Preventing and Curing Employee Burnout

www.employer-employee.com/Burnout.html

Tips and strategies for preventing burnout for managers and employees.

Relaxation Direct

www.relaxationdirect.com

Stress fundamentals, stressful lifestyles, and strategies for coping with stress.

"Seven Ways to Beat Stress"

http://magazines.ivillage.com/goodhousekeeping

Article on managing stress, the mind-body connection, and stress reduction.

TheSpark.com's Stress Test

http://test.thespark.com/stresstest/

Stress test and guide to "losing it all."

Stress Exhaustion and Burnout

http://members.farmline.com/stress/management/exhaustion.htm

Detailing the pressure to perform and difficulty with relaxation and sleep.

Stress Help Center

www.stresshelpcenter.com

Stress-coping, self-help techniques of relaxation, yoga, visualization, sound nutrition, and perceptual reframing.

Stress and the Immune System

www.econ.uiuc.edu/~hanko/Bio/stress.html

Paper by Hannah Koenker regarding the effects of stress on the immune system.

Stress Management

http://tc.unl.edu/stress

Includes the fundamentals of stress management, an educational tutorial, and class notes from University of Nebraska's Stress and Tension Reduction course.

Stress Management Information and Methods

www.smartway.org.uk

Find out your stress levels and how to reduce them using self-help methods and stress-reduction products, including visualization and relaxation techniques.

Stress Management and Lifestyle Resources

www.davidposen.com

Resources and articles on stress management techniques, stress management tips, and workplace stress management.

Stress Reduction Articles

www.articles911.com/Stress_Related_And_Mental_Health

Index of free Internet articles on stress management, relaxation techniques, and coping techniques.

Stress-Related Problems

www.helpforfamilies.com/stress1.htm

Description and advice for parents.

Suite 101: Relieving Stress

www.suite101.com/welcome.cfm/relieving_stress

Articles related to finding ways to unstress in crisis and in everyday life.

Twilight Bridge—Coping with Stress

www.twilightbridge.com

Articles and online discussion forum on counseling and stress.

Virtual Library—Stress

www.clas.ufl.edu/users/gthursby/stress

Books, resources, guides, e-mail lists, newsgroups, journals (electronic and print), professional organizations, and stress management directory, including commercial products.

Why Be Nervous?

http://rbt.tripod.com/index-5.html

Explores nervousness and stress and suggests that there is a link to low blood sugar.

Wildmind

www.wildmind.org

Gives practical advice on how meditation can help manage stress.

The Work-Stress Network

www.workstress.net

An organization that aims to educate and raise awareness of work stress and to improve legislation on health, safety, and employment rights.

Working Stiff STRESS-O-METER

www.pbs.org/weblab/workingstiff/stressometer/index.html

Stress quiz that tests your work environment stress levels.

Index

A

anxiety, vs. urgency, 126–128
appointments, missed, 76–77

B

breathing, 22–23
builders, 137
burnout: defined, 2–3; stages of, 3; test for, 3–8
burnout-inducing stress, 11–12

C

call blitzes, 194–195
career: moving forward in, 138–140; stages of, 134–137; turning point in, 129–133
coaching meetings, 159–160
coaching plans, 163–168
cold calls: calling blitz for, 194–195; practicing, 65–66; removing stress from, 176–177; scheduling, 36, 65
communication tips, 117–118
commute, 42
compensation structures, 174–175
competitors, 76
complacency, 77
computer bulletin boards, 111
contacts, finding alternate, 53–54
contributors, 135
conversion ratios, 64–65
creative stress, 11–12, 123–125
customer comment cards, 110
customer service, 100–103
customers: feedback from, 109–112; listening to, 101; retaining, 104–108; staying in touch with, 101–102, 109–112

D

daily numbers, 58–60
delegating, 29, 144
diet, 16–17, 18–19

E

e-mail, 111
easy sales, 77
employee surveys, 111
enthusiasm, 151–153
exercise, 16, 20–21

F

feedback, customer, 109–112
fight-or-flight syndrome, 14
flow, 45–50
focus groups, 110
follow-through, 142
forecasts, developing, 185–190
friendships, 30–31, 145

G

goal setting, 154–158
goals: changing, 132; setting specific, 154–158; setting uninspiring, 79–81; sharing, 131–133

H

habits: evaluating your, 83–84; instilling new, 67–70; transition curve for, 169–171
Hirsch, Samson Raphael, 44
honesty, 72–73, 74

I

income goals, 58–60
income performance, 139–140
initial meetings, 88–91

L

leaders, 136
lies, 74
lies, sales, 72–78
lifestyle changes, 16
limit setting, 28–29

M

mail surveys, 111
managers: asking for help from, 51–52; keeping in loop, 117–118
meetings: initial, 88–91; time frames for, 95–97
mentors, 161–162
mornings, 38–39

N

needs-based selling, 74–75
negative images, 13–15
no: learning to say, 28–29; understanding meaning of, 55–57
novices, 135
numbers, daily activity, 58–60
nutrition, 18–19

O

online resources, 204–207

P

performers, 136
personality traits, 141–143
perspective, 24–25
physical activity, 20–21
presentations, preparing for, 95–99
prioritizing, 144–145
productive selling days, 85–87
professionalism, 122–125
Prospect Management System: categories of, 180–184; effectiveness of, 191–193; using the, 185–190
prospecting: discipline for, 32–34; need for, 73; removing stress from, 176–177; scheduling, 36

prospects: vs. customers, 100–103; initial meetings with, 88–91; interacting with, 89–91; missed appointments by, 76–77; replenishing, 61–63, 64–66; requests for presentations from, 95–99; sure thing, 77; training your, 119–120

R

recruitment, 150–153
rejection: taking personally, 75; tenaciousness in face of, 142
rejection trap, escaping from, 55–57
relaxation techniques, 16
relaxing, time for, 26–27
resource stage, 107–108
resources, 204–207
retention programs, 172–173
rewards, 26–27
Rivers, Mickey, 25

S

sales career: moving forward in, 138–140; stages of, 134–137
sales forecasts, developing, 185–190
sales goals, 79–81
sales, misconceived ideas about, 72–78
sales projections, unrealistic, 113
sales relationship, stages of, 104–108
sales routine, based on needs, 74–75
sales slumps, 61–66
sales training, 172–173
salespeople: enthusiastic, 151–153; as investments, 178–179; personality traits of, who don't burnout, 141–143; plateauing, xi; reality check questions for, 196–197; recruitment of, 150, 150–153; as resources, 104–108; self-obsessed, 92–94; tech people and, 114–116; turnover rates of, x
scheduling. *see also* time management: cold calls, 36; grouping similar activities, 35–37
self: lies told to, 72–78; rewarding, 26–27; taking care of, 144–145; taking time for, 38–39
seller stage, 106
sleep, 17
slumps, 61–66
smiles, 44
stress: burnout-inducing, 11–12; creative, 11–12, 123–125; inevitability of, 9–10; response to, 10–11; tips for dealing with, 16–17; using, 10
stressful situations: constructive responses to, 69–70; getting perspective on, 24–25; immediate reactions to, 13–16; recognizing, 13–16
success rituals, 40–41
supervisors. *see* managers
supplier relationship stage, 106
support networks, 30–31

T

target companies, finding different point of entry for, 53–54
technical team, 114–116
telephone surveys, 110–111
telesales professionals, 198–203
tension. *see also* stress: tips for dealing with, 16–17
thank-you correspondence, 112
time management, 16, 35–37, 82–84
training programs, 172–173
truths, creating own, 146–147
turnover rates, x

U

urgency: vs. anxiety, 126–128; instilling sense of, 119–120

V

vanity selling, 92–94
vendor relationship stage, 107
volunteer work, 17

W

Web pages, 111
work environment, 43–44
work habits, 32–34
worry, 24–25

About the Author

Stephan Schiffman is a certified management consultant and the founder of D.E.I. Management Group, a global sales training company. Mr. Schiffman has helped more than 500,000 professionals become more successful through a variety of selling and coaching programs. He is the country's pre-eminent expert on sales prospecting, and the author of many popular business titles, including *Cold Calling Techniques (That Really Work!)*. To learn more about Stephan Schiffman or D.E.I. Management Group, call 1-800-224-2140 or visit *www.dei-sales.com*.

Online Learning Resources from D.E.I. Management Group

Visit *www.dei-sales.com* and take advantage of the following online courses:

- Cold Calling Techniques: How to Get More Appointments
- Don't Wait to Hear "No"
- Getting to "Closed"—Prospect Management
- High-Efficiency Selling
- Seven "Make It Happen" Questions You're Not Asking
- Sixteen Keys to Getting More Appointments
- The Top Ten Sales Mistakes (and How to Avoid Them)
- Using Questions to Accelerate Sales

And, especially for managers:

- The Monday Morning Meeting